EDUCATOR'S GUIDE TO
Catholic Curriculum

LEARNING FOR 'FULLNESS OF LIFE'

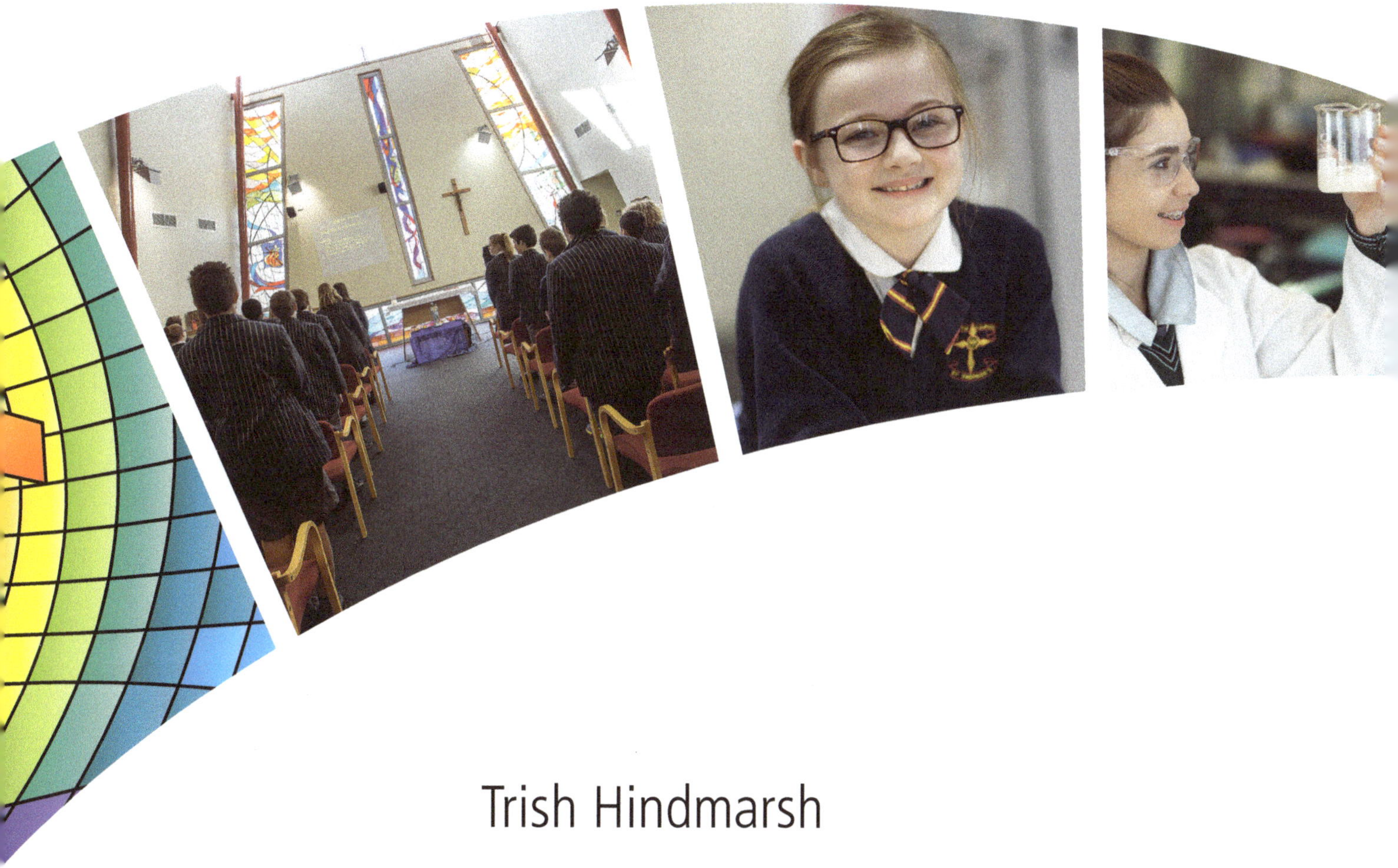

Trish Hindmarsh

The *Educator's Guides*

The Mission and Education Project of BBI-TAITE (The Australian Institute of Theological Education) presents a series of Guides to serve the educational mission of Catholic schools in Australia and beyond. The Guides, each dealing with a specific area, introduce educators to ways in which mission and education may be integrated in the life and work of Catholic educators and students. The mandate given to the expert writers who create these Guides is to tap into the best available treatments of mission and also to ground their work in quality practice.

It is with great pleasure that I present the second of the *Educator's Guides* by Dr. Patricia Hindmarsh. Her work is essentially a celebration of the splendid efforts educators from across Australia and New Zealand are making to integrate faith and the learning areas of the curriculum.

Those who allow themselves to be attuned to the project which Jesus began with his small band of followers so long ago – to make present and to nurture God's dream for creation - will recognise the genuine feel for that dream which is reflected in these pages.

Therese D'Orsa
Professor Mission and Culture
BBI-TAITE
Commissioning Editor Mission and Education Project

VAUGHAN PUBLISHING
A joint imprint of BBI – TAITE & Garratt Publishing

Published in Australia by Vaughan Publishing
32 Glenvale Crescent, Mulgrave VIC 3170

A joint imprint of Garratt Publishing and BBI - The Australian Institute of Theological Education.

Copyright © 2017 Trish Hindmarsh

All rights reserved. Except as provided by Australian copyright law, no part of this publication may be reproduced in any manner without prior permission in writing from the publisher.

Cover design and typesetting by Eggplant Communications.

The author and publisher gratefully acknowledge the permission granted to reproduce the copyright material in this book. Every effort has been made to trace copyright holders and to obtain their permission for the use of copyright material.

Special thanks to the Tasmanian Catholic Education Office, and indeed the students and parents from Tasmanian schools, who granted permission to use the images that you will see throughout this book.

'Cover of Australian Catholic Bishops' Social Justice Statement 2015–16'. Image used with permission of the Australian Catholic Social Justice Council.

The publisher apologises for any errors or omissions in the above list and would be grateful if notified of any corrections that should be incorporated in future reprints or editions of this book.

ISBN 9780987306043

National Library of Australia Cataloguing-in-Publication entry

Creator: Hindmarsh, Patricia, author.

Title: Educators Guide to Catholic Curriculum: Learning for Fullness of Life / Trish Hindmarsh.

ISBN: 9780987306043 (paperback)

Subjects: Catholic Church--Education.
    Education--Religious aspects--Catholic Church.
    Catholic teachers.
    Catholic schools.
    Church and education--Catholic Church.
    Christian education--Catholic Church.

Nihil Obstat: Reverend Monsignor Gerard Diamond MA (Oxon), LSS, D.Theo
    Diocesan Censor

Imprimatur: Monsignor Greg Bennet, MS STL VG EV
    Vicar General

Date: 25 May 2017

The *Nihil Obstat* and *Imprimatur* are official declarations that a book or pamphlet is free of doctrinal or moral error. No implication is contained therein that those who have granted the *Nihil Obstat* and *Imprimatur* agree with the contents, opinions or statements expressed. They do not necessarily signify that the work is approved as a basic text for catechetical instruction.

Contents

Introduction		1
Chapter 1	Being 'Catholic'	6
Chapter 2	Jesus at the Heart	10
Chapter 3	Faith in Action	13
Chapter 4	A Catholic Curriculum	18
Chapter 5	Teachers reflecting	26
Chapter 6	The Humanities, Social Sciences and The Arts	31
Chapter 7	The Sciences, Maths, Health/PE	39
Chapter 8	Vocational Education	45
Chapter 9	Religious Education	49
Conclusion		56

Acknowledgments

Many teachers and educators have contributed to this guide, either directly through their research and professional practice, or indirectly through their influence as champions of Catholic education. I wish to acknowledge the following people particularly:

Professor Therese D'Orsa and Dr Jim D'Orsa, whose seminal work, *Catholic Curriculum: A Mission to the Heart of Young People* (2012), laid the academic foundations in theology, mission studies and education for this guide. Their vision, encouragement, practical advice, and extensive experience as teachers and educational leaders, have all greatly influenced work in this field of education over many years. Their perseverance and foresight have made this guide possible.

Other educational leaders who have supported this project at some level include:

- Ms Susan Apathy, Deputy Chief Executive Officer, New Zealand Catholic Education Office
- Dr Paul Sharkey, Catholic Education Melbourne
- Dr Anne Wenham, St Stanislaus College, Bathurst
- Dr Sandra Harvey, Catholic Education Office, Hobart
- Mr Tony Brennan, Catholic Education, Tasmania
- Mr John McGrath, National Catholic Education Commission
- Ms Pam Betts, Executive Director, Catholic Education Brisbane
- Dr Dan White, Executive Director, Catholic Education Office Sydney
- Dr Peter Hamill, Director, Broken Bay Catholic Schools Office
- Professor Jim Gleeson, Australian Catholic University, leader of the 'Identity and Curriculum in Catholic Education' project, which has been a fruitful source of examples in this work.

The following schools and agencies have contributed to the guide through the examples included, which illustrate creative ways of developing and resourcing curriculum implementation in a Catholic educational context.

- Loyola Catholic Trade Training Centre, Western Sydney
- St Columban's College, Caboolture
- St Anthony's Primary School, Alexander Hills
- Holy Spirit School, Bray Park
- La Salle College, Cronulla
- Kavanagh College, Dunedin New Zealand
- St Peter Chanel Catholic Primary School, Smithton
- St Mary's College, Hobart
- Guildford Young College, Hobart
- St Virgil's College, Hobart
- St Brigid's Catholic School, New Norfolk
- St Brigid's Catholic School, Wynyard
- St Anthony's Catholic School, Riverside
- St Patrick's College Launceston
- St Peter Chanel Catholic School, Smithton
- Columban Inter-faith Dialogue Centre, Sydney
- Caritas Australia
- Tasmanian Catholic Justice and Peace Council

Reverend Professor Denis Edwards, Australian Catholic University, for his valuable feedback.

Jill Miles, Catholic Education Office, Hobart, for her professional assistance with the choice of photos.

Regina Lane, publisher for Vaughan Publishing provided invaluable professional advice and support in the pre-publication phases and has been responsible for the layout and presentation of the guide.

Introduction

Its task (the Catholic school) is fundamentally a synthesis of culture and faith, and a synthesis of faith and life: the first is reached by integrating all the different aspects of human knowledge through the subjects taught, in the light of the Gospel; the second in the growth of the virtues characteristic of the Christian. *The Catholic School* #37

One afternoon while I was sitting in the hairdressing salon, a conversation between two young mothers caught my attention. 'I know you're happy with the Catholic school and I'd really like Alice to go there too; it seems to have a great reputation, but I'm concerned they might influence her with too much religion'. This alerted me again to the reality … we live in a largely secular age, and yet Catholic schools remain an attractive option for many families. What signs of hope and opportunities for a meaningful life can the Catholic school offer in these times of crisis, when faith is no longer a taken-for-granted aspect of our culture?

In my experience, most parents are looking for a school they hope can equip their children to succeed in a high tech, competitive society. They expect the curriculum will prepare their children to find a meaningful and fulfilling place in the world. But above all, they want their children to be happy, to value their young life, relate well to others, make sensible decisions and be engaged in their learning, even finding joy in new knowledge and skills, while steadily growing in self-awareness, self-discipline and maturity.

Parents are also aware that our culture offers many false, even destructive attractions and promises. They hope the school can help prepare their children to develop the capacity to recognise which are the noxious 'weeds' and which the life-giving 'seeds' to be found in their culture as they grow into young adults.

Teachers also have high hopes for students. They know that the relationships and sense of community teachers develop with students, together with the way they plan and deliver the curriculum are critical if they are to foster in young people what Pope Francis described as the harmony between 'the heart, head and hands'.[1]

Catholic schools have an intrinsic faith dimension, as the mother in the salon recognised. A Catholic school exists in response to Jesus' mission to bring the Good News of life, love and hope to all humanity. The Catholic school by its very nature aspires to be a place where the lessons taught and the community life are 'enlivened by the spirit of the Gospel', with Christ at the centre, every day and in every activity. This is at the heart of the 'identity' of the Catholic school.

So it is that the Catholic school is dedicated to offering students learning opportunities that develop their God-given gifts and dignity, empowering them to understand and appreciate the true meaning and values of life and the part they are called to play in building the Kingdom of 'justice, peace, love and beauty', as Pope Francis describes in 'A Prayer for our Earth' from *Laudato Si,* 'A Prayer for our Earth', #246.).

It seems to me that 'these theological understandings' that underpin the Catholic school are not far removed from the hopes of parents, who do not for the most part use 'churchy' language but at the deepest level want the 'best' for their children. The Catholic school is built on the belief that Jesus Christ came to offer 'the best' for every person. He announced, 'I am the Way, Truth and Life', (John 14:6). The challenge is to bring this understanding alive for staff, parents and students within the very busy, focussed context of the 'real' world in which the school exists. It requires reflection, prayer and above all respectful dialogue and communication between all parties. The challenge is to be a Catholic school that it true to its deepest 'Identity'.

Religious Education Expo, Hobart, 2012.

Catholic identity and Curriculum

'Catholic identity' has been explored in the *Educator's Guide to Catholic Identity*, (Paul Sharkey 2015)[2]. Sharkey introduces several essential elements that go towards building the Catholic identity of what is increasingly being referred to as a 'recontextualised' Catholic school.

These elements include the centrality of Jesus, the 'frontier' nature of our times, shared liturgy and prayer, pedagogy, curriculum, data analysis, 'ecological conversion', staff formation, family, parish and school relations, charity and justice, befriending difference and 'doing theology'. When a school community consciously works to develop these elements in a unity inspired by an ever-renewed understanding of the mission of Christ, the school can be both relevant to contemporary educational needs and truly 'Catholic'. In contemporary research terms, it might be recognised as a 're-contextualised' Catholic school.

Curriculum

Each of the elements of Catholic identity listed above has its own challenges and deserves detailed analysis. In this guide it is the element of the 'curriculum', the mandated set of key learning areas to be taught, that is my specific focus.

The potential of the formal curriculum to be a means of grace for students has always excited me. It has been a sacred experience to see eyes light up in a Science or English class as students learn and develop, discovering both the strengths and shadow sides of culture and gaining insights into the mysteries of the natural world. I have been privileged to know many teachers who bring to their classroom a sense of what Pope Francis calls the 'joy of the Gospel'[3], teachers recognised not only as excellent professionals, but also as 'evangelisers' (bearers of the 'Good news' of Christ). They recognise each student as a precious child of God, and bring the Good News of freedom and hope alive through their enthusiasm and commitment to their areas of teaching expertise.

Catholic schools, in this case Larmenier in Launceston, publicly proclaim their identity.

It is important to consciously plan for a high quality curriculum that takes full advantage of Catholic life and a Catholic worldview. Much work has been done already towards a 'Catholic' approach to curriculum.

In the 1990's I was part of a team in Sydney Catholic Education who developed a curriculum project titled 'A Sense of the Sacred'. The project identified key Catholic understandings and associated Gospel values, relating these to the prescribed courses of study in English, Science, Business Studies, Economics, Legal Studies and Mathematics, and suggesting an extensive resource listing and practical examples of implementation to assist teachers in Catholic secondary schools[4]. In this guide I set out to explore how such connections can be drawn in twenty-first century professional teaching practice. This guide features some examples of how a 'Catholic' approach to curriculum is emerging in in various Australian and New Zealand Catholic schools and systems.

Foundational to this guide is the exploratory work of Therese and Jim D'Orsa, *Catholic Curriculum: A Mission to the Heart of Young People* (2012). The work offers an in depth study of how the mission of Catholic schools is expressed through the curriculum, by means of a dialogue between faith and culture. The book outlines key principles that underpin a Gospel-based approach to curriculum, inviting reflection on the historical, anthropological, theological and philosophical developments that have shaped the diversity of cultures in our own times and the challenges and opportunities these developments present for Catholic educators.[5]

This guide aims to support teachers by bringing a practical, on-the-job approach to this significant academic work.

Can there be a 'Catholic curriculum'?

This question has challenged educators responsible for the implementation of the public curriculum in a Catholic context, prompting them to ask related questions such as, Can the public curriculum ever justifiably be referred to as a 'Catholic' curriculum, without becoming problematic? Will reference to a 'Catholic curriculum' place the integrity of the curriculum at risk of manipulation?

On one level, one could argue that a 'Catholic hospital' or a 'Catholic school' are descriptors well accepted in society; the popularity and track record of these institutions demonstrate that they are able to carry out fully the agreed purpose and standards society has set for health and education in a hospital or school. Catholic hospitals and schools are subject to the same public scrutiny and accountability as are government ones. They must follow the same universal regulations and policies. However, they have their own expression, a 'Catholic' expression of these requirements.

Similarly, it can be argued that the Catholic worldview that influences these institutions can also be applied to implementation of the public curriculum, as a 'Catholic curriculum'.

We do not speak of 'the' Catholic curriculum any more than we speak of 'the' Catholic school or hospital, out of respect for the fact that local cultures influence their unique development, including the ways in which faith comes alive within them.

A 'Catholic curriculum' will necessarily emerge from the cultural context in which the public curriculum has been developed. In the case of 'Catholic' hospitals, there will rightly be some critique of the policies and methods by which public health needs are delivered if these do not reflect the spirit of the Gospels and Catholic faith.

Similarly, Catholic schools need to meet expectations that they will deliver the curriculum in a way that is faithful to their mission as instruments of the Church to bring human development and the new life of Jesus to all, through formal learning. Hence, we can reasonably speak of a 'Catholic curriculum'.

As Therese and Jim D'Orsa point out, the content of any curriculum is limited; none of us know the future for which students are preparing, but we do know that the future will be shaped, not only by 'human action' but by 'the creative action of God in the world'. Hence for a curriculum to be future-oriented, it requires courageous leadership to 'promote a deep, intelligent and meaningful relationship with Jesus, which becomes the axis on which all else turns'. [6]

Larmenier Catholic School, St Leonards.

Scope of the guide

In Chapters 1, 2, and 3, the guide looks firstly at some of the features that distinguish the Catholic faith: its worldview and values, Christ its heart, its rich heritage and mission in the today's world.

In Chapter 4 we explore the possible scope and meaning of a specifically 'Catholic curriculum' that aims to link faith and spirituality with the subjects taught.

In Chapter 5, we introduce a reflective process of 'doing theology'. This is a simple method students and teachers can engage in as a way to enrich their planning and their learning, empowering them to make decisions based on sound evidence and spiritual reflection, building reflective habits that can last a lifetime.

In Chapters 6, 7, 8 and 9, the guide addresses each of the broad disciplines that make up the public curriculum, with special reference to subjects developed through the national Australian Curriculum. We explore and illustrate how these disciplines can be brought into a dialogue with faith, culture and life.

In Chapter 6, we consider the Humanities, Social Sciences and the Arts.

In Chapter 7, we turn our attention to the Sciences, Maths and Health/PE.

Chapter 8 considers a Catholic approach to Vocational Education and how learning a trade is an aspect of preparation for engagement in full and meaningful life.

Chapter 9 discusses the central role of Religious Education in a Catholic school and how it can be related in a dialogue of learning with the other key learning areas to create an 'ecology' of learning.

Built into each section are some reflective points and relevant quotations for shared discussion. The hope is that teachers, in reading the guide, will engage in individual or group reflection about how to plan and deliver a genuinely Catholic approach to curriculum. This is always a work in progress, gathering impetus as understanding grows. Where practical examples are lengthy, a relevant extract is included and the full version referenced online.

I hope that this guide both honours some of the great work being done towards 'a Catholic curriculum' and opens up exciting future possibilities for teachers to explore new pathways and share their learning both locally and globally.

Developing a genuinely 'Catholic' approach to curriculum is a sharing in God's mission to the world, and a response to the Church's call for a 'new evangelisation'. The curriculum has an essential part in making visible Jesus' promise of 'abundant life' through every aspect of student learning, (John 10:10).

> *I have come that they may have life and have it to the full.*
>
> John 10:10

CHAPTER 1

Being 'Catholic'

The Catholic school tries to relate all of human culture to the good news of salvation so that the light of faith will illumine everything that the students will gradually come to learn about the world, about life, and about the human person. Declaration on Christian Education # 1 Vatican Council II

It is always a challenge to articulate clearly what being 'Catholic' actually means and implies. As a lifelong member of the 'tribe', I still struggle to find words to express both the privilege and the challenge of belonging. We know that the Eucharist is the 'source and summit' of the Christian life and the sacraments are vital sources of God's grace. We are fired by the sheer beauty and strength of Christ's mission of love to the whole of creation. We believe the Holy Spirit empowers the Church to share in that mission.

Today, the struggle to be authentically 'Catholic' is being lived out in the shadow of great scandals and rapid change in human consciousness. Schools, as one of the 'good works' of the Church, have a vital role in modelling what a genuinely 'Catholic' community can offer society.

Teachers in Catholic schools know that the 'Catholic identity'[7] of their school is of critical importance to its educational integrity. Other terms that are sometimes used are 'Catholic ethos', 'Catholic character' or Catholic worldview'. Christ, his mother Mary, and the Saints are enshrined in the names of Catholic schools: St Mary's, St James, Mary MacKillop, Sacred Heart etc. The Eucharist is celebrated and the Catholic liturgical year guides the prayer life of the Catholic school. Teachers need to be able to recognise and take advantage of the Catholic nature of their school to enrich their teaching.

Catholic faith can help find answers to many questions impinging on a person's life, Biblical questions such as: Who am I? Why am I here? What is life all about? Who is God? Why do some people seem to suffer so much? How can they be better served? Why was I created? Why should I move from self-centredness to other-centredness? How can this be done? What constitutes a life well lived? Or questions about society: Who is benefitting from these political and economic arrangements? Who is identifying the marginalised and bringing them into the centre of consideration in the way society (or this school) is being led and managed?[8]

Bishop Putney, former Bishop of Townsville, in describing 'Catholicity' for Catholic schools in the Queensland context (Putney, 2008, pp. 18-20) drew on the definition of North American Religious Educator Thomas Groome in his seminal book *Educating for Life*. Groome wrote that Catholicity involves:

> … a positive anthropology; a sacramental consciousness; commitment to relationship and community; appreciation for tradition; cultivating reason for wisdom of life; and the cardinal commitments of fostering holistic spirituality formation in social justice and inculcating a catholic worldview … (Groome, 1998, p. 427).

For Catholics, that 'sacramental consciousness' is most fully celebrated in the Eucharist when the community gathers in memory of Christ to celebrate his life-giving death and resurrection, and to praise and thank God for the gifts of creation.

In the 1990's the Sydney Catholic Education Office wanted to link Catholicity and the curriculum. To this end, the resource, *A Sense of the Sacred,* was developed for secondary schools. The first challenge was to describe what 'Catholicity' looks like and what light it can shed on English, Science, Legal Studies,

Being Christian is about much more than beautiful places of worship; it involves a living community of faith seeking to follow Jesus Christ.

Mathematics, History, Geography etc. Five 'big ideas' related to a Catholic worldview were identified. These include the following understandings, closely related to those identified by Groome above, and drawn from the work of Rohr and Martos:

1. The Sacredness of all Creation: All God's creation is good and holy; all is gift of love from the God who is Love.

2. Human Dignity: The Kingdom Jesus announced, knows no borders, but is totally inclusive and respectful of all, especially the poorest and the weak. Human beings are 'God's work of art' (Ephesians 2), made in God's own image and likeness.

3. Communion with all: we form part of the great family of God, a community of life, celebrating God's love and sharing God's mission to make real in our world the Kingdom of God Jesus announced, which is a way of peace, freedom and love for all creation.

4. Cultural Transformation: We are called to work for justice, peace and ecological responsibility for all, challenging whatever is not life-giving in our culture and affirming all that is.

5. Reconciliation and Hope: God is always ready to forgive sin and failure and a better future is always possible.[9]

We know that a living faith cannot be reduced to disparate elements, to words and concepts. However for the sake of clarity, each of the key understandings described above can be teased out through identifying and describing related values and concepts, as outlined for example in the following table.

Five Foundational Catholic understandings	Associated concepts and values
The Sacredness of all Creation 	**Grace:** God's gift **Unity:** The hope that all may be one in God's Kingdom, regardless of creed, race, social class **Ecology:** recognition of the interconnection of all of life **Respect:** Honouring all created things as gifts from God not to be taken for granted **Stewardship** (Conservation): Cherishing creation. Recognising that no-one has absolute power over God's earth **Joy:** Awareness of the beauty and bounty of creation **Justice:** the gifts of the earth are to be shared equitably among all **Awe and wonder:** Capacity to marvel at God's gifts of creation **Mystery:** A sense of the transcendent
Human Dignity 	**Sacredness of life:** Seeing God as the origin and creator of all life and expressing gratitude for the gifts of life **Human Rights:** All people have the right to a dignified life, free from oppression, and to have their basic human needs met. **Social Justice:** There needs to be a right ordering of relationships in society, an exercise of power that can be life-giving for all **Liberation:** Freedom from all that oppresses **Moral responsibility:** Ability to make choices that reflect the ethics of the Gospel
Communion	**Living tradition:** An inherited faith, constantly refreshed through the sacramental life of the Church and its response to the signs of the times **Conflict resolution:** Resolving conflict in a way that respects individual and communal needs **Community:** A group of people with shared vision and commitment to mutual service **Family:** The basis of society and church, reflecting God's creative love **Interfaith Dialogue:** Honest dialogue with people from other faiths, respecting similarities and differences and leading to greater social cohesion. **Service:** Loving attention to the needs of others following Jesus' foot-washing example and in response to one's vocation
Cultural transformation 	**Conversion:** A change of heart in response to God's grace **Structural Change:** Identifying the root causes of injustice in the world and working to bring about positive change **Solidarity with the Poor:** Acting with and on behalf of the poor to bring justice. Living one's personal lifestyle conscious of global inequity **Inculturation:** Bringing the Gospel message alive so that culture is affected by the Good News, 'right down to its very roots' (*Evangelii Nuntiandi*, 20) **Openness:** Receptivity to new ideas, other cultures and disciplines **The Common Good:** Total human well-being

Five Foundational Catholic understandings	Associated concepts and values
Reconciliation and Hope	**Reconciliation:** Bringing those estranged together, through God's grace, in mutual understanding and forgiveness
	Cross-Cultural Understanding: Positive interaction with other cultures for mutual enrichment
	Empowerment: Giving people power to act in their own right
	Vocation: One's life work carried as a response to God's will
	Hope: An enduring trust in God's goodness that can sustain faith

Table 1. Adapted from the original *A Sense of the Sacred* project, Sydney Catholic Education Office, 1994

These concepts and values have direct relationship in many cases to content in the prescribed school curriculum, and can be used as touchstones to identify possible links between curriculum content, Kingdom values and religious faith. The concepts are powerful, and have the potential to help teachers and learners grasp reality and clarify thinking to create meaning for their lives. A complete expression of the official teachings of the Catholic Church can be found in *The Catechism of the Catholic Church* (1992).

group activities

1. Imagine you are about to interview parents enrolling their child for the first time in a Catholic school. How would you respond to the question, 'So really, what's different about a Catholic school?'

2. Using Table 1, and referring to a unit of work you are currently planning to teach, identify some concepts and values listed that would be relevant. Plan strategies that could give 'wings' to those concepts. Share your work with a partner or small group of teachers.

CHAPTER 2
Jesus at the Heart

The heart of Catholic faith and life is the person and mission of Jesus Christ, Word made flesh and teacher of life par excellence. As the Gospels tell us, 'He taught as one having authority'. (Mark 1:28)

Jesus announced his mission in Luke 4:18. He was sent to 'bring the Good news' to all who suffer… the poor, the blind, the imprisoned, the stranger. As he was leaving his disciples, he told them to bring that same Good news of God's love for all, to 'the whole of creation', to 'the ends of the earth' (Mark15:16), that is to say, to every culture in every time. The Gospel truth is to be announced. Jesus' way is to be lived. The 'abundant Life' (John 10:10) he promised is for all. The mission of the Catholic Church and of the Catholic school as a ministry of the Church is to be part of this mission of Jesus to every culture in every time. What a privilege and a challenge!

'Culture' in this context is not be confused with 'high culture' (the arts, architecture etc). Culture in this context means the sum total of all the structures and organisational arrangements, the underlying narratives and traditions that belong to a particular people, nation or group. God's mission, which is shared by the Catholic Church (and by extension, the Catholic school), is to bring the Good news of salvation alive in every aspect of our own culture.[10] The day-to-day teaching that happens in classrooms is a powerful aspect of that mission as teachers open up the many facets of culture with students through teaching and learning in each of the subject areas.

Meeting Jesus in the Scriptures

The scriptures are a resource that transmits the 'Good news' of Jesus Christ who is the Light of the world. We want our students to 'see the Light', not just by acquiring knowledge and skills, but also by growing in wisdom.

In working with Catholic educators in relation to the Catholic identity of the school, I have invited teachers to reflect on the question: 'What is a favourite scripture quote that inspires you?', and then to explain in a sentence what that means to them. These are some of their responses:

A favourite scripture quote	Personal interpretation
'I have called you by name: you are mine' (Isaiah 43:1).	We are called and loved by God, warts and all
'Can a mother forget her infant, be without tenderness for the child of her womb? Even should she forget, I will never forget you'. (Isaiah 49:15).	God knows and loves me. That's an incredible thought.
'Whoever wishes to come after me, must deny himself, take up his cross and follow me'. (Matth. 16:24)	We can draw spiritual strength to endure suffering.
'If I, therefore, the master and teacher, have washed your feet, you ought to wash one another's feet'. (John 13:14)	We are called not to be served, but to live in service of each other.

A favourite scripture quote	Personal interpretation
'Father, forgive them; they know not what they do'. (Luke 23:34)	We are called to forgive even those who hurt us the most.
There is 'a pearl of great price' (Matth 13:45) and a 'treasure buried in a field' (Matth 13:44), symbols of the Kingdom of God.	The really important things in life are worth searching for.
'When I see the heavens the work of your fingers, the moon and stars that you set in place, what are humans that you should be mindful of them?' (Psalm 8:4)	The whole cosmos is God's loving creation. I marvel at it and cherish earth as my home.
'I give you a new commandment: Love one another. As I have loved you, so you also should love one another'. (John 13:34).	Genuine love is the foundation for human happiness, for me and for humanity.
'All power in heaven and on earth has been given to me. Go, therefore, and make disciples of all nations, baptising them in the name of the Father, and of the Son, and of the holy Spirit, teaching them to observe all that I have commanded you'. (Matth 28:18)	The Church's mission is to bring God's life and grace into each new time and place.
'Then God said, "Let the earth bring forth all kinds of living creatures: cattle, creeping things, and wild animals of all kinds..."God saw how good it was'. (Genesis 1:24)	The earth is God's gift, the 'garden' that nourishes us all, and we need to care for it through responsible human stewardship.

As Catholic educators, through the inspiration of faith and the depth of spirituality alive in our schools, we have a 'treasure, not made of gold. In earthen vessels, wealth untold'. (Based on 2 Corinthian 4:6-7). Our teachers and students can come to know the 'treasures' of the Gospel; we can offer them 'wealth untold' through the riches of our faith tradition, illuminating school-based learning in all its facets.

Jesus, teacher extrordinaire

Jesus could not help himself; he was a teacher and taught casts of thousands during his short public life. It was his vocation. He taught on hillsides, out of boats, in the local synagogues and in the temple, over dinner, in people's homes, on the dusty tracks, and from the executioner's cross. His teaching captivated audiences and so affected minds and hearts that humans have been prepared to believe and live by the lessons he taught during the twenty centuries since. He was described as one who taught with 'authority'. That authority came from being true to his deepest identity. He knew who he was. He described himself as the Way, the Truth and the Life. Jesus taught using compelling stories, parables and the treasures of the tradition he had inherited. His message was radical and uncompromising. He made it clear that he had a great subject to announce, the Kingdom of God. That was his curriculum.

Christ taught as 'one having authority'.

Mark 1:28

Parker Palmer tells teachers, 'In a culture of technique, we often confuse power with authority, but the two are not the same. Power works from the outside in, but authority works from the inside out. [11] Palmer claims that it is the deepest identity, the inner self of the teacher, the sense of vocation and wonder that makes a difference. Just as Jesus could not but teach about life, truth and the way to God, so Palmer explains how the inner core of the teacher responds to subjects that fire their imagination. He writes, 'Geologists are people who hear rocks speak, historians are people who hear the voices of the long dead, writers are people who hear the music of words.'[12] To teach is to be passionate about our vocation, driven by an inner light fanned by a thirst to know what Palmer calls 'great things', the 'subjects around which the circle of seekers are always gathered'. The Catholic school is a 'circle of seekers', modelled on the circle of disciples Jesus gathered around him. They had been invited to, 'Come and see', they responded and became seekers of the truth, learning 'great things' from a passionate teacher who loved them and was in love with his subject, the Kingdom of God. They were enthralled. This is why Jesus the teacher is at the heart of the Catholic school.

activity

1. Where do you find your passion as a teacher? What subjects, what 'great things' are dear to your heart?

2. Who is Christ for you? How does your school community celebrate the presence of Christ day-to-day and share his teaching?

CHAPTER 3

Faith in Action

Cultures do not remain static; our world is evolving every day, constantly responding to change: migration, globalisation, natural disasters, new scientific approaches to health and industry, or changing sociological approaches to family, economics, religion and community development.

Many Australians are alarmed as the worldview of their nation, seen as egalitarian and offering a 'fair go' for all, appears to be evolving towards a more exclusionist and individualistic society in response to global pressures. Political developments globally trending towards isolationism and the erosion of long fought-for structures to protect human rights and the environment present immense challenges.

Grandparents and parents are given to commenting on how much the world has changed in their lifetime as the old certainties have been replaced by new worldviews and lifestyles. The narratives of faith that sustained them and developed their beliefs and attitudes have given way to secular narratives of economic progress and social success. Many young people are themselves becoming alarmed by the high-tech, rapid-paced world in which they are expected to function, a world often devoid of spiritual nourishment and adverse to human flourishing. For many Australians, the closest thing to faith in today's world seems to be the remembrance of heroic deeds of war, celebrated for example through the Anzac tradition.

Faith that is relevant

Catholic faith constantly re-expresses itself to bring fresh hope and wisdom to the world in these changing times. Today's teachers of History and Geography can take courage from Pope Francis' teachings in *Evangelii Gaudium* (2013) and *Laudato Si* (2015), which address many of the economic and ecological challenges humanity faces. The Australian Catholic Bishops' Statement for Social Justice Sunday 2015, 'For Those Who Come across the Seas', is another powerful learning resource, challenging Australia to be open and generous towards those seeking asylum from war and persecution, making a Gospel-based response to one of the toughest issues of our times. As a Catholic educator, I was proud and heartened by these documents, buoyed by hope and spurred to action.

Many people want their children to share the riches of their own and their parents' life-giving faith, even though faith may have become somewhat obscured for them by the pressures of life in a secularised culture.

We know that new times call for new approaches to announcing the Good News of salvation. The Church is always called to renewal, as are individuals. Likewise, the Catholic school is called to renew itself in the ever-changing contexts of learning if teachers are to be hope-filled, convinced bearers of the Gospel for our students in this challenging century.

The term 'recontextualising' (adapting to meet the needs of new contexts, new times) is often used in relation to ministries of the Church, including education. The Church, the parish and the school all need to be 'recontextualised' to remain fresh and relevant in today's world, while also remaining faithful to the Gospel and the faith tradition we have inherited from our forebears.

Vatican Council II recognised this and embraced the 'hopes and fears' of the age as the concern of the Church. Pope Francis recognises in a refreshing, life-giving way the need for new approaches. He speaks in a way people understand about issues that concern them, for example, the 'migrant' and 'asylum seeker' global phenomenon; discrimination based on a person's sexuality; family life; the 'frontiers' emerging from scientific research that can alter the very building blocks of nature.

These pressure points and questions arise in classrooms in Catholic schools. Students in our schools come from diverse backgrounds; they represent the broad spectrum of ideas and beliefs, ethnic background,

The Social Justice Statement of 2015 brought the light of faith to shine on the pressing issue of refugees.

special needs and sexual orientations that are typical of our culture. Teachers, open to Christian ideals and ethics, need to teach the curriculum in a way that is both responsive and realistic in taking account of the actual world their students live in.

For discussion

In your experience, what are the 'hot button' issues that arise in class for students? Share some ways in which these issues can be dealt with on a day-to-day basis as they arise?

A Catholic worldview recognises that the seeds of the Gospel can be found in positive aspects of our secular culture, for example, through volunteers working for charities, in loving relationships, in the defence of human rights, in positive approaches to human health and in the rule of law.

The Church also recognises that every culture has a shadow side that needs critique and positive change, for example, prejudice that excludes those who are 'different', excessive consumerism, over-emphasis on celebrity status, a lack of care for the most marginalised, an ecologically unsustainable economic system.

The mission of the Church and of the Catholic school is to bring the light of Jesus' Gospel to empower students as they study and learn to recognise and embrace authentic love, justice, truth and human virtue, wherever they are found, and to recognise and reject the contrary.

Faith in Action

At some stage the pure Mathematics we teach students needs to become 'applied' to real life situations and challenges if it is to become useful in building bridges, balancing the books or guiding scientific research. Similarly with Catholicism. The Church's mission and its teachings, the life of faith, needs to be 'applied' in business and social life. For our students, the subjects they study are gateways to culture; faith can enlighten their learning.

Two practical 'tools' the Catholic Church offers can be invaluable in bringing faith alive in the classroom: one is the art of 'Dialogue', and the other the body of 'Catholic Social Teaching'.

Dialogue

Recent Catholic teaching on mission and evangelisation, and now Pope Francis, have identified 'dialogue' as a crucial method for bringing the Gospel alive and carrying out Jesus' mission to the world.

In practice, dialogue means people coming together and endeavouring to understand one another by sharing life and experience; by talking issues through from the position of seeking to understand the other; by working together to achieve common goals, and by praying together. In dialogue there is no privileged position, because people meet as equals. This may be why Pope Francis is so keen to remain open to the real challenges of the world, to meet people from all walks of life, listening to their hopes and fears, structuring meetings that enable him to hear the needs of the poor and oppressed, and prayerfully responding in collaboration with the affected parties.

Teachers in Catholic school classrooms are in a unique position to engage in dialogue with their students through the learning process. The importance of dialogue is seen for example in the ways teachers approach new scientific, religious and health issues that constantly surface on social media or are directly related to the curriculum.[13]

Classroom connections: Dialogue in Practice

An example of inter-faith dialogue in action is seen in Chapter 9 where Catholics, Muslims, Jewish, Mormon, Buddhist, and Hindu young people celebrate their shared humanity and respect each other's faith tradition as they walk the Tasmanian wilderness together.

Dialogue between science and faith is illustrated in Chapter 7 through the growing understanding of the cosmos. Faith acknowledges God as creator, and science explains how this has happened through the billions of years of evolution. With both worldviews, the scientific and the religious, working together over centuries, a new clarity and understanding of the truth about the origins and nature of all that exists becomes possible.

An example of primary students engaged in a dialogue of learning is described in Chapter 7 at St Anthony's Primary School in Alexander Hills, Queensland. Here, Religious Education and the other subjects of the curriculum are planned to work together to develop values and attitudes, knowledge and skills, inspired by Catholic Social Teaching, implementing the prescribed curriculum in ways that both respect its intentions and make meaningful the rich and positive teachings of the Catholic Church.

At the edges: Catholic Social Teaching

Catholic Social Teaching is recognised throughout the Christian world and in wider society as a powerful means of responding to the signs of our times. In the 1890's, the particular concern for Pope Leo XIII was 'the rights of workers'. Since then this body of teaching has been developed in response to the great challenges of war and peace, human rights, economic justice, poverty, migration, employment, disintegration of cultures and family life. These teachings are a modern expression of the Gospels, bringing Christ's teaching into dialogue with contemporary culture.

The great themes of Catholic Social Teaching are named by Caritas Australia with teachers and students in mind, and include: The Common Good; Dignity of the Human Person; the Preferential Option for the Poor; Solidarity; Subsidiarity and Participation; Stewardship of Creation.[14]

The Australian Catholic Social Justice Council (ACSJC) is an agency set up by the Church to 'promote research, education, advocacy and action on social justice, peace and human rights, integrating them deeply into the life of the whole Catholic community in Australia, and providing a credible Catholic voice on these matters in Australian society'. Both the ACSJC and Caritas publish a wealth of material teachers and students can use to grow in understanding of justice and peace issues related to the curriculum.[15]

Catholic Earthcare Australia is a related Church agency whose vision is for 'an ecologically sustainable and resilient Australia, where Catholic communities play an active part in the holistic care of social, human and environmental ecology'. Catholic Earthcare offers a wealth of research and practical resources schools can access to address the 'Sustainability' Priority of the curriculum. The resource *On Holy Ground: an Ecological Vision for Catholic Education* is used in individual schools and systems for this purpose. The Catholic

Earthcare Australia ASSISI project is also available for schools as an integrated approach whereby the total school culture and each of the key learning areas can lead students towards ecological understanding and responsibility. The Catholic Church is committed to seriously addressing ecological responsibility and the realities of climate change in a way that is accessible and practical for those involved in education.[16]

Vatican Academies

Many Catholics do not know that in Rome, the Pontifical Academy of Science and the Pontifical Academy of Social Sciences carry out significant scientific and humanitarian academic studies, applying world class research to help address pressing global issues. For example, the 'End Slavery' project against human trafficking was personally instigated by Pope Francis. As he explained:

> I have stated several times that these new forms of slavery – human trafficking, forced labour, prostitution, organ trade – are very serious crimes, a wound on the body of contemporary humanity. The whole of society is called to grow in this awareness, especially with regard to national and international legislation, in order to prosecute the traffickers and redirect their unjust gains to the rehabilitation of victims.[17]

For discussion

How do you think students and teachers of subjects such as Geography, Legal Studies, Business Studies, Science and Religious Education can be supported by the work of the Catholic agencies cited above?

Catholic education authorities respond

Catholic educational authorities who administer systems of schools express their understandings of how Catholic belief and life can affect curriculum through guiding documents and curriculum projects. Some examples are:

1. The 'Brisbane Catholic Education Learning and Teaching Framework' (2012), provides a Catholic interpretation to inform the academic disciplines. The framework is a valuable resource to guide Catholic educators as they plan to implement the 'given' curriculum. It offers a faith-based interpretation of the dignity of the human person, a holistic approach to learning, an approach to creation as God's gift, and an understanding of a living faith tradition that reveals God's love. The framework rests on a Catholic understanding of the following disciplines:

   - An Anthropology that describes how humans are God's creation, made with great dignity 'in God's image', with all that this belief implies.

   - An Epistemology that claims that human beings best learn in a holistic way, with heart, mind and hands working together.

   - A Cosmology that sees all creation as sacred and humans as stewards of creation.

   - The Christian Story and Tradition that is enshrined in scripture and Church teaching, leading humans to understand God's plan for Creation [18]

2. Brisbane Catholic Education has created a project founded on these five key understandings, that integrates Catholic beliefs and values with the Australian Health/PE curriculum. This project is described in Chapter 7.

3. In New Zealand, Catholic schools engage in a national system to review their authenticity as Catholic schools. Schools are required to do an annual internal review of their 'Catholic Character' and an external review every few years to ensure that, 'as well as developing learning and skills, the whole curriculum inculcates Catholic attitudes and values'.[19]

The document 'Virtues and Values in New Zealand Catholic Schools' supports the development of 'Catholic character'. As a response to the Vatican document, *The Catholic School* (1977) 'Virtues and Values' describes the Catholic school as 'a privileged means of promoting the formation of the whole person', leading to 'the acquisition of values and the discovery of truth… the bringing forth of the power of Christian virtue by the integration of culture with faith and of faith with living…For a Catholic school the values it promotes must be sourced from the Gospels, particularly the parables of Jesus'.[20]

Kavanagh College in Dunedin, drawing on this document, is an example of how 'values sourced from the Gospels' can be translated into the total life of the Catholic school. Over three years the whole college participated in processes of formation and consultation to distil four Gospel values, as a blueprint for living for the college community: Respect, Service, Truth, and Justice, values to apply in every aspect of college life. [21]

4. The various bishops' 'Charters' of Catholic education that guide Catholic schools, currently in use for example in the dioceses of Sydney and Hobart.

5. The four 'Touchstones' of Edmund Rice Education Australia (EREA)

6. The charism, values and beliefs associated with schools influenced by a religious order, for example, Presentation, Josephite, La Salle, Loreto, Mercy, Marist and others.

These examples illustrate how Catholic education is committed to retain, interpret and strengthen the 'Catholic' nature of its schools, faithful to Christ and his Church, while serving families who must live in a largely secularised culture.

For discussion

1. If you were founding a brand new Catholic school, how would you plan to develop and foster its Catholic character?

2. In what ways can a Catholic educational 'authority' eg a Catholic Education Office, support its member schools to be authentically Catholic?

CHAPTER 4
A Catholic Curriculum

From the nature of the Catholic school also stems one of the most significant elements of its educational project: **the synthesis between culture and faith**. Indeed, knowledge set in the context of faith becomes wisdom and life vision….The various school subjects do not present only knowledge to be attained, but also values to be acquired and truths to be discovered. *The Catholic School on the Threshold of the Third Millennium #14*

Asking the questions

Can there be a 'Catholic' approach to curriculum? Can a Catholic school culture, founded on Jesus and his Gospel, make a difference to the way Mathematics, English, Sciences and Technologies, Geography, History, Economics, Vocational Education or the Arts are taught?

Can students be inspired by the values of the Gospel as they grapple with new information, respond to data and evidence through class dialogue, acquire new skills and make decisions related to their learning?

Can the classroom bring the Gifts and Fruits of the Holy Spirit alive in the hearts of learners? For example, can Wisdom, Courage, Understanding, Knowledge, Piety, Love, Peace, Joy, Goodness, Patience, Perseverance quietly take root and grow as students engage in Legal Studies, Business Studies, Technology and Design, Health and Physical Education, Drama or other learning areas? These are exciting questions.

A 're-contextualiased' Catholic school?

Contemporary Catholic schools around the world are asking: What does the 're-contextualised' Catholic school look like? In other words, how can we create genuinely 'Catholic' school environments in the context of a secular, technological age? How can the Gospel be brought to life anew in this time and this culture within the milieu of the Catholic school? How can learning programs, based as they are on a public curriculum, which is itself a creation of secular culture, serve the needs of a specifically faith-based Catholic education? How can the so-called secular subjects be instruments of the Good News of Jesus for individual and global flourishing? How can students be equipped to critique and reject those aspects of their culture which are not conducive to human and planetary health, and hence are contrary to the will of a loving God for creation? Equally, how can students learn to recognise what is good and life-giving in their culture? How can students be encouraged to develop their God-given gifts through the subjects they study and see their future life and work as a vocation of love and service?

For discussion

Consider the quotation from Church teaching at the head of this chapter. What examples can you share from your own teaching that have resonated with the claim, 'The various school subjects do not present only knowledge to be attained, but also values to be acquired and truths to be discovered'?

Larmenier Catholic School, St Leonards.

In summary, how can the curriculum help students to make sense of their life and their world?

I believe it is the dream of most parents that the Catholic school would support their child in becoming an adult who can rejoice in the gifts of life, face its challenges with courage and a well-developed conscience, finding purpose and fulfilment through their life vocation. That is also the hope of the Church in setting up systems of Catholic education to serve the needs of young people. The curriculum plays a key role in realising these hopes.

Pioneering 'Catholic curriculum'

The Bishops in colonial Australia recognised early the need to create specifically 'Catholic' schools in the face of the catchcry, 'free, secular and compulsory' that led to the establishment of state-run, secular schools under the Education Act of 1871. The Bishops recognised that Catholic schools needed to offer a holistic education, a distinctive blend of faith and culture. They stated in 1862:

> Catholics do not believe that the education of a child is like a thing of mechanism that can be put together bit by bit. Now a morsel of instruction on religion and then of instruction of secular learning- separate parcels. We hold that the subjects taught, the teacher and his faith, the rule and practices of the school day, all combine to produce the result that we Catholics consider to be education.[22]

Powerful words, still relevant a century and a half later. From the earliest days in the colonies, priests had sought out dedicated Catholic lay people to run simple bush schools, teachers committed to the mission of the Gospel to bring 'Good news' to the poor and the isolated through curricula that provided basic Arithmetic, Spelling, Reading and Writing, together with a knowledge of Catholic faith and values that

The first school run by the Sisters of Our Lady of Sion in Sale.

Religious Education Expo Hobart, 2014.

would enable them to live good and productive lives in a society hostile to Irish Catholicism.

During the century following the Education Act, the Catholic Bishops invited numerous religious orders to come to the colonies to set up systems of schools based on Catholic beliefs and offering high quality schooling.[23] From the 1860's Mary MacKillop and Father Julian Tenison Woods had already founded Catholic schools for the poor across Australia, delivering a curriculum that would enable neglected and poor children to take their place in society.

Contemporary Catholic schools in Australia belong to one of the world's great Catholic educational systems. They are staffed now almost exclusively by lay people, building on the legacy of the religious orders, always seeking ways to offer a curriculum that remains faithful to both the Gospel and the needs of the students of our own times. The contemporary curriculum is complex, the times characterised by technological and human challenges. There are no simple answers from the 'penny catechism', as there were in my childhood, no easy solutions to today's big questions.

However, the Church, especially in the light of Vatican Council II, continues to seek ways to 'recontextualise', that is, renew and re-express, the faith, in response to evolving culture/s, ever alert to address the signs of our times. Catholic faith can illumine all areas of human life and learning. The curriculum can be an instrument for good in this regard.

Catholic schools that fail to offer the fullness of the Christian message to students, via all areas of the curriculum, risk contributing to the 'split between faith and culture' that is identified by the Church as the 'drama of our times'.[24]

reflection

1. Ask an older Catholic what their childhood experience of Catholic schooling was like for them.

2. Referring to the quotation on pg 19 from the Catholic Bishops in the 1860's, to what extent do you think their curriculum vision continues in Catholic schools today?

The Gospel and curriculum

As we saw in Chapter 1, a Catholic worldview is based on the belief that humans are made in God's image, that the cosmos is the expression of a loving God, that Jesus is 'the way, the truth and the life' (John 14:6), whose Spirit breathes in everything that exists. These beliefs are a treasure trove for the teacher working in a Catholic school setting.

Teachers can set up conditions for dialogue between faith and the culture as they offer engaging pedagogy and open up the curriculum with students. Teachers can pose questions, stimulate responses, build in reflective practices, choose relevant resources, make connections between disciplines, as they open up a particular area of study and recognise its potential to make visible the Kingdom of God. In other words, teachers can see the key learning areas as means of 'evangelising culture right down to its very roots'[25], through linking learning with the Gospel message.

Students bring to school their own view of the world, formed by the family and the wider culture in which they live. They continue to form their worldview through the various subjects studied. The Catholic school provides access to the living tradition of faith as every day in learning spaces students enter into dialogue, raise questions, learn new skills and come to their own knowledge of the world, shaping their futures.

Outcomes for life

Teachers are conscious of the skills, knowledge and understandings they hope exiting students will take with them from school. In a Catholic context, they may well ask some searching questions about the effectiveness of thirteen years of schooling as a preparation for a reflective and well-lived life. For example:

- Will our Economics class know that Pope Francis has seriously questioned the prevailing global economic model on the grounds that it neglects the poor and exploits the earth?

- Will students of Geography come to connect the importance of ecological responsibility and human dignity for urban design and food production, as Pope Francis' has done in his encyclical *Laudato Si*?

- Will English students be aware that language empowers them to communicate well and help bring about appropriate social change?

- Will they understand that literature can shed light on the strengths and weaknesses of human nature and its longing for true fulfilment?

- Through Mathematics, can students come to appreciate the elegance of the laws that govern the cosmos, God's creation?

- Through data analysis can they begin to understand something of the injustices that flow from inequality of access to the world's resources, entrusted by God for all to share?

- In Health and Physical Education classes, will students come to understand the sacredness of their own body as a unique gift from God, and the responsibility they have to care for human well being, their own and others?

Teachers in Catholic schools are rising to the challenge to make learning links between faith, life and culture through the key learning areas of the formal curriculum. A number of examples of their work are included in the later chapters of this guide.

> **reflection**
>
> Consider the questions posed above. Formulate your own reflective question/s linking the day-to-day curriculum you teach with the spiritual and faith development of your students. Be as honest as you can.

'Doing theology'

When teachers and students are engaged in reflective practice that includes a faith dimension and a sense of the spiritual they can be said to be 'doing theology' at the grass roots, a process we explore more fully in the next chapter.

The total life of the school

Of course we know that the total life of the Catholic school, sometimes referred to as the 'hidden curriculum', its Catholic 'character' or 'identity', underpins and supports everything that happens, especially formal curriculum delivery. It is taken for granted here that the culture of the school (the sum total of its arrangements, policies, organisation and experiences) is foundational.

We know that students flourish best as learners in a school community permeated by an atmosphere of Gospel freedom and love.

Some approaches

In Australia, some system authorities that govern and support Catholic schools are seeking ways to experiment with and trial the challenge for a 'Catholic' approach to curriculum in their schools. Two examples follow.

Pioneering new approaches

1. In Tasmania, teachers in Catholic schools have been invited in their curriculum planning cycle to take into account an agreed fourth Priority area, identified as 'Catholicity', together with the existing three Priorities already included in the Australian national curriculum model (Indigenous, Asian and Sustainability).

   Further, teachers are encouraged to consider an additional General Capability, 'Acquiring Wisdom', to sit with the existing General Capabilities within the Australian Curriculum. These include Literacy, Numeracy, ICT Capability, Critical and Creative Thinking, Personal and Social Capability, Ethical Capability, Intercultural Understanding.[26]

2. In Queensland, the project, 'Identity and Curriculum in Catholic Education', is jointly sponsored by the Archdiocese of Brisbane, Queensland Catholic Education Offices, the Sisters of Mercy, Edmund Rice Education and the Presentation Sisters, in partnership with Australian Catholic University.

   This action/research project works with teachers to trial how Catholic Social Teaching can be integrated into the various curriculum areas. Examples of this approach in progress through secondary Science, and primary Visual Arts, Geography and Health/PE, are shared through the following chapters.[27]

Curriculum mapping

Teachers are accustomed to mapping the curriculum to include essential elements. Table 2 can be used as a 'check list' to decide which faith-based concepts and values may be relevant to a unit of work teachers are planning.

Catholicity: Concepts and Values	Related Catholic Social Teachings	Curriculum Elements
1. Sacramentality of all Creation Grace, Unity, Ecology, Respect, Stewardship, Joy, Justice, Awe and wonder, Mystery **2. Human Dignity** Sacredness of life, Human Rights, Social Justice, Liberation, Moral responsibility **3. Communion** Living tradition, Conflict resolution, Community, Family, Interfaith dialogue, Service **4. Cultural Transformation** Conversion, Structural Change, Solidarity with the Poor, Inculturation, Cultural Critique, Openness, The Common Good, Vocation **5. Reconciliation and Hope** Reconciliation, Cross-Cultural Understanding, Empowerment, Vocation, Hope	Human Dignity The Common Good Option for the Poor Solidarity Subsidiarity Stewardship of Creation	**General Capabilities** Growing in Wisdom Literacy Numeracy Information and communication technology (ICT) capability Critical and creative thinking Ethical understanding Intercultural understanding Personal and social capability **Priorities** Catholicity Sustainability Aboriginal Asian

Table 2. Linking Catholicity with curriculum elements

It is assumed here that in a Catholic school, 'Catholicity' can be considered a 'Priority' for all subject area, and 'Acquiring Wisdom' a 'General Capability'. Further it is assumed that potentially these can be developed through any subject, across all disciplines.

activity

Consider a unit of work you are planning or teaching at present. Refer to Table 2 and identify faith-based and curriculum elements that are relevant to this unit. Design some strategies to include those elements in the learning cycle for this unit.

For their encouragement, teachers in a Catholic context need also to be conscious, as St Paul put it, that they but plant the seeds; it is God 'who gives the increase' (1 Corinth. 3:6). As we know, learning is a complex, deeply personal process with a spiritual dimension. However, teachers can help plant seeds of goodness and wisdom, and water them! For example:

Classroom connections

- In vocational education, the word 'vocation' has a spiritual dimension that both teachers and students can depth. A teacher of Hairdressing can help students to understand how the skills they are developing can equip them to be of genuine 'service' and to build people's 'self-respect', just as Jesus did in his lifetime, and called his followers to do. Likewise, a teacher of Construction or Engineering could consciously plan to help students understand that shaping the built environment can be a form of genuine 'service', more than just a job, requiring good 'stewardship' of the earth's resources, and making a contribution to the 'common good', building the God's Kingdom of love and peace on earth.

- An English teacher preparing to teach a novel such as *To Kill a Mockingbird* **or** *The Book Thief* could be conscious of the values and concepts associated with Human Dignity…'sacredness of life', 'human rights', 'social justice', 'liberation', and 'moral responsibility'. Students can come to recognise a character such as Atticus Finch as a Jesus of Nazareth type figure, who unflinchingly faced the consequences of his commitment to peace, justice and inclusion, forgiving enemies, a model of integrity and non-violence for the locals in a racist small town in the Deep South of the United States.

Priorities and Capabilities: A Gospel view

Another way of approaching curriculum planning in a faith-based school context, taking the Australian Curriculum as an example, could be to look at the actual 'Priorities' and 'General Capabilities' that are mandated, and explore how they can be enriched with scriptural/spiritual/ faith beliefs, insights and understandings. (All other school curricula around the world will have similar elements that can be depthed in the light of faith).

We look first in turn at the General Capabilities:

1. Literacy and Numeracy: In a Catholic school context, these capabilities are not to be considered as merely pragmatic skills to strengthen the economy. They can be recognised as competencies that are basic for human participation in society and tools for building the Kingdom of God on earth. Education has always been a missionary work of the Church, a way of fostering human flourishing, from the founding of the great monasteries as centres of learning in the Dark Ages, to the universities and schools founded in the Middle Ages, which have continued to exist and develop ever since.

2. (ICT) capability: The Church appreciates that the social media of communication can be positively used for the 'common good'. Pope Francis shares aspects of the Good News daily through social media and says that the digital media can be used for good as a 'culture of encounter'.

3. Critical and creative thinking: Catholic Church teaching on education consistently condemns indoctrination and encourages openness to truth, beauty and goodness wherever and however they can be discovered and expressed.

4. Personal and Social Capability: The Gospel teachings related to loving God and our neighbour, forgiving enemies and living in community are sustained by the sacramental life of the Church and expressed in outreach to others.

5. Ethical understanding: Christians are called to respect and keep the 'Great Commandment', founded on love of God and love of neighbour. Ethical and moral ways of behaving apply to every aspect of life. Without such standards, cultures fall into corruption and chaos.

6. Intercultural understanding: St Paul wrote to the Galatians, 'There is neither Jew nor Greek, slave nor free, woman or man; all are one in Christ Jesus' (Gal. 3:28). The Catholic Church is universal and open to all cultures. Recent popes have encouraged and engaged in interfaith dialogue.

Similarly, each of the Australian Curriculum Priorities can also be interpreted in an enriched way in the light of faith. For example,

1. Sustainability: Pope Francis has written for the world a powerful encyclical, 'Laudato Si' explaining the sacredness of the earth, 'Our Common Home' and how we need to be in relationship with each other and with the earth. Recent popes, bishops and religious orders have strongly addressed ecology.

2. Aboriginal perspective: Pope John Paul spoke to Aboriginal people at Alice Springs, acknowledging to them that, ' *for thousands of years you have lived in this land and fashioned a culture that endures to this day…The silence of the Bush taught you a quietness of soul that put you in touch with another world, the world of God's Spirit*'[28]

3. Asian Perspective: The great religions of Asia are honoured in Catholic teaching about respect for other faiths, and interfaith dialogue. The Jesuit missionary, Matteo Ricci, in bringing Catholic faith to China, respectfully related with its ancient culture.

Aboriginal studies at Sacred Heart Catholic School, Geeveston.

Teacher reflection

These processes of deepening our approach to the curriculum require teacher reflection (discernment). It could be said that, in making choices and decisions as to what to include or emphasise in a unit of work, the teacher is engaging in a sacred task. The process is sometimes referred to as 'doing theology' because it requires asking faith-related and spiritual questions that add depth to learning and help students and teachers find meaning for their lives through the subjects they study.

The following chapter introduces a simple, time-honoured reflective process of discernment that can be applied to take curriculum planning to another level.

For discussion

1. Share an opportunity you have had to make a connection to spirituality or faith in your daily classroom teaching (other than in a Religious Education lesson).

2. In your experience, which subjects can be most naturally connected with or draw enrichment from faith/spiritual understandings? Illustrate with some examples.

St Therese's Catholic School, Moonah.

CHAPTER 5
Teachers Reflecting

We are living in an information-driven society which bombards us indiscriminately with data- all treated as being of equal importance- and which leads to remarkable superficiality in the area of moral discernment'. In response, we need to provide an education which teaches critical thinking and encourages the development of mature moral values. Pope Francis, *Evangelii Gaudium, # 64*

Reflective practice

Many teachers working in a faith context have found it a 'natural' part of their decision-making and planning to include a reflective step asking themselves questions such as:

- 'What would Jesus have to say about this? How can I engage the students/staff in a way that respects their God-given dignity?

- Isn't there something in Catholic Social Teaching that can enrich this topic?

- Are there passages in scripture that speak to the theme of this novel, poem/ or play?

- How can I as teacher (of Literacy, Science, English, Food Studies etc) connect with the Religious Education program?

In asking such questions teachers can be said to be 'doing theology', raising what some teachers refer to as 'God questions' in relation to the curriculum. They are not thereby interfering with the integrity of the particular curriculum subject area, but rather exploring the possibility of enriching learning experiences to include a spiritual or a faith dimension. There would be no point in 'forcing' connections artificially of course.

As one Maths teacher explained to me with a bit of a twinkle in the eye, when preparing a series of lessons on Quadratic Equations for a Year 9 class, there is not a strong ethical or religious component immediately recognisable in the pure algebra as such, at least not with this class right now! Of course some might dispute this, revelling in the sheer beauty of complex algorithms and mathematical theories as descriptors of the harmony in God's universe. However, this teacher told me she would take the conscious decision to honour the human dignity of her students both in the way she related to them, and in how she grouped students in class to better respond to their varying learning needs. She pointed out that to do this successfully as a Maths teacher requires a reflective approach on her part to curriculum planning, not to mention the assistance of daily prayer for patience and wise judgment!

Teachers and curriculum leaders are no strangers to reflective planning. In preparing units of study, they customarily engage in a reflective cycle, posing questions to determine the needs of the students, choosing the knowledge, values and skills to be developed and creating strategies to be introduced during the 'learning cycle '. Implementation is followed by evaluation, and the cycle begins again.

In planning for a 'Catholic' approach to curriculum, there are additional questions to consider: *What light can faith and a deep spiritual sensitivity, add to this learning sequence? How can I as teacher prepare myself to teach with humility and passion?* These questions take reflective practice to another level. Parker Palmer maintains it is what he refers to as the 'great things' (the truths, the knowledge, to be discovered through the subjects studied) that can captivate both teacher and student. These 'great things', these treasures of learning, can be discovered and appreciated when there is room for reflection.

The Curriculum Planning Cycle in a Catholic School Context

1. ASKING:
- What are my students' needs? Academic, Developmental, Spiritual?
- How do I know? (evidence?)
- What does the curriculum require?
- What do Catholic faith and values have to contribute?
- How do I prepare myself professionally and spiritually to teach this unit?
- Do I have genuine passion and knowledge to teach the subject?
- What advice would Jesus the Teacher have for me and my students?

2. DESIGNING LEARNING EXPERIENCES AND TASKS.
- Respecting students' dignity as made in God's image, by planning for their participation and dialogue.
- Choosing Resources, including, where relevant, Catholic Concepts and Values, Catholic Social Teachings, lessons from Church history or inspiring life models. (Refer to Table 2)
- Identifying potential links with aspects of the RE curriculum

3. THE CLASSROOM PROCESS
- Being conscious that this learning process has the potential to support students to grow in the Gifts of the Holy Spirit.
- Using 'Dialogue' as a respectful way to engage students.
- Sharing passion for the 'great thing' that is being explored through this curriculum subject (Parker Palmer's phrase)
- Encouraging the values of the Kingdom, (love, peace, justice, courage…) in classroom interactions and through the subject being taught

4. EVALUATING
- Asking: How well did the learning experience go, academically, but also spiritually? From my viewpoint and the students'?
- Did the students and I observe signs of the Gifts of the Spirit at work in this time of learning?
- Was there any direct relevance to Christian faith and Gospel teaching and if so, how did students respond?
- Was there an atmosphere of inquiry, dialogue, excitement, insight and gratitude about new learning?
- Did I or my students have an opportunity to grow in wisdom? How was that recognisable in their responses or mine?
- Were students' lifestyle choices influenced in any way by their learning?
- Was there any natural opportunity for a prayerful response that emerged as this unit unfolded?

With acknowledgement of the work of Helen Timperley's curriculum planning model, found in Timperley, H. (2011, May). *Using student assessment for professional learning focusing on students' outcomes to identify teachers' needs*. Retrieved from www.education.vic.gov.au/Documents/about/…/timperleyassessment.pdf

For discussion

Refer to the diagram and text above regarding 'Reflective Practice'.

How useful and practical for teachers in Catholic schools is it to include steps in the curriculum planning cycle that consciously take faith and spirituality into account?

Discernment

In posing spiritual questions within a reflective process, teachers are not only 'doing theology', but engaging in a form of *discernment* in the traditional Catholic sense (as understood and taught for example in the Ignatian spirituality of the Jesuits).

Discernment is a tool for acquiring the spiritual gift of Wisdom through reflection on reality in the light of faith, and coming to a sound decision that is expressed in positive action. Catholic educators can engage in discernment as individuals or in a group. They can model the processes with students at many points of the curriculum. Discernment can become an enduring and invaluable life skill. It is a prayerful process, and Catholic schools are places of prayer, both public and private. It would be a sad day if Catholic schools ceased to deeply reflect on the learning programs they present to their students!

Students also need reflective processes (discernment) to help them come to wise decisions in challenging situations in their young lives. For example, for a student to persevere with a difficult subject choice, or to bring insight to their analysis of a work of fiction, a level of reflection is required on their part if they are to come to positive, and even life-changing judgments and decisions. A Catholic school environment can help students to ask spiritual and faith-related questions in coming to both deeply know and love themselves and to make many important decisions about their study, health, relationships or futures.

Pope Francis is calling all Catholics to exercise this form of reflective thinking to discern how Christ, through His Spirit working in us, would approach the small and great issues we daily face. Such issues can include: family life; forming relationships; the expression of love between humans; lifestyle choices; ecological responsibility; the divide between rich and poor; refugees; the inclusion of all in the Reign of God.

Steps in 'doing theology'

The process described below is offered as a practical way of engaging in discernment, of 'doing theology', at the grassroots level. The process involves a series of steps that build on each other, each with suggested guiding questions. As acknowledged earlier, many teachers and school staffs already engage in reflective practice, but a specific format can help hone reflective skills to include a spiritual/ faith dimension.

The reflective process can be seen as always spiralling upwards, with new knowledge and wisdom building for us on past knowledge and wisdom, like Jesus, who 'grew in wisdom and grace', (Luke 2:52)

Another way to remember the sequence of the process is to *See* (the reality), to *Judge* (the reality), and to *Act* (on that reality) 'See, Judge, Act' became the catchcry of the Young Christian Workers' Movement in the 20th century, and formed the basis for the formation of many Catholics who went on to become leaders in public life and formed movements that changed society. With practice, the process becomes second nature, establishing a lifelong habit of reflecting before taking action.

Students wore the badge and learnt the 'See, judge, act' process as members of the YCS (Young Christian Students Movement).

For discussion

In the light of the 'See, judge, act' method outlined above, recall a time when you practised discernment in arriving at an important decision for (a) your life, and (b) your teaching practice.

Reflective Process: See, Judge, Act

Step 1. Exploring the Situation:

What is happening here? What does the data say? What do we know already? What do I/we understand about the situation so far? Who is involved? What standards, criteria, expectations are at play here?

Step 2. Deepening Understanding:

What needs to be happening if good outcomes are to follow? What does the spirit of our school charism (or motto) have to contribute to this reflection? How do I/we think Jesus would approach the situation? Is there a scriptural quote that springs to mind in this context? Are the themes of Catholic Social Teaching relevant here? Can I/we pause and pray for guidance from the Holy Spirit for a few moments? What concepts and values associated with Catholicity are relevant to this issue, scenario or unit of work? What are accepted best standards and practice in relation to this issue? Have we named the heart of the matter?

Step 3. Coming to Decision and Action:

What is the best outcome/decision I/we can take as a result of our reflection? What specific action needs to follow? How can we make this action happen in practical terms? Who will be responsible to see it through? How can I/we revisit this process to make sure my/our decisions remain effective and relevant?

Reflection at whole school level

A process of theological reflection is needed at the wider school level also, for example in curriculum planning groups or in refreshing the school's vision, mission and strategic direction. As some of the case studies we share in this guide illustrate, there are school and system leaders who are already very good at practising 'grassroots theology', engaging in deeply reflective processes.

The following scenario outlines the experience of a small rural Catholic school in reviewing and refreshing its Vision and Mission through a process of Christian discernment.

Whole school discernment: St Peter Chanel Smithton, Tasmania

1. Seeing - Describing the situation.

A facilitator engaged the staff and parent representatives in a process of sharing responses to the question, 'What are the characteristics of our school'? 'How would you describe our school?

2. Judging - Deepening Understanding

Staff reflected on official Church teachings regarding Catholic education and also on Pope Francis' speech to Catholic educators. (November, 2015).

3. Acting - Decision and Action:

Staff concluded that the Mission and Vision of the school needed to be refreshed.

The decision was taken to rewrite the Vision and Mission as one document that would reflect the character and mission of the school as discerned through the previous two steps and incorporating feedback from a formal validation process the school had recently undertaken. They would also plan to incorporate the ecological aims of Catholic Earthcare Australia. A small group of 'writers' was appointed to draft the document, and a realistic timeframe set for completion.

Civics and Citizenship

A further example in a senior secondary context to illustrate how discernment is needed can be seen when eighteen year old students become eligible to exercise their democratic right to vote for the first time. They need to ask: Who are the candidates? What do they stand for? What do I believe is important for the country? How do I know who is best placed to serve the community? How will I cast my vote?

The Tasmanian Catholic Justice and Peace Commission issued some guidelines for senior students for the 2016 federal election, drawing on guiding principles from Catholic Social Teaching as criteria to judge the various policies being put forward. Students were encouraged to reflect on which candidates seemed to be in tune with the principles of Justice for all, Human Dignity, the Common Good, Care for the Earth and the Preferential Option for the Poor, as candidates publicly commented on policy issues such as a fair tax system, employment, aged care, disability support, treatment of refugees and asylum seekers, environmental responsibility.

The electoral guidelines were offered as a resource for teachers to use with Year 12 in a seminar situation. The desired outcome was that students would engage in a reflective approach with their teachers prior to the election and hopefully be better placed to grow towards responsible citizenship, developing capability in 'critical and creative thinking', 'ethical understanding' and 'personal and social capability', with the enrichment of a Christian perspective.

In Chapter 7, there is a further classroom example of discernment happening in the context of Science, as a class group of students respond to the discovery of 'Gravitational Waves'.

A lifetime habit

What an asset for life, to be able to draw on a reflective process that could save ourselves and our students from some regrettable, ill-considered decisions, and, if used consistently to form a reflective habit, could guide a lifetime of wise decision-making. In fact, reflection is a time-honoured way to discern what the theologians term, 'God's will', for us, and for the world, in the here and now. Discernment links contemplation and action, work and prayer, enabling us to pray as Jesus taught us, 'Thy will be done, on earth as it is in heaven'.

For discussion

1. Share examples of some scenarios in curriculum planning that could be enriched through engagement in a process of reflection as outlined above.

2. Share an experience you have had when the 'Catholic Christian' nature of your school made a specific difference to a decision reached by students or staff.

3. Share some examples of how you have observed students gaining insights and growing in wisdom as they engage in their formal learning.

CHAPTER 6

Humanities, Social Sciences and the Arts

The increased attention given to science and technology must not lead to a neglect of the humanities: philosophy, history, literature and art. Since earliest times, each society has developed and handed on its artistic and literary heritage, and our human patrimony is nothing more than the sum total of this cultural wealth. Thus, while teachers are helping students to develop an aesthetic sense, they can bring them to a deeper awareness of all peoples as one great human family. The Religious Dimension of Education in a Catholic School, # 60

In this chapter and those following, we share some practical ways in which the various disciplines can be approached in a Catholic school, inspired by the life and teaching of Christ. We begin with the Humanities. Their significance is acknowledged in the extract from Catholic Church teaching above.

Our focus here will be on Language, History, Geography, Economics and The Arts.

English and Language Studies

Through English and other language studies, students learn to read, write, speak and listen effectively. They learn to engage meaningfully with literature and the media. Through these studies students are also able to prepare for active participation in building the Kingdom of God, as they:

- participate more proactively in their culture through literature and the media, becoming more informed, articulate and creatively expressive

- learn to identify good and evil through what they read and discuss, discerning the positive and negative aspects of circumstances and characters

- relate to others and communicate positively, to 'love one another', with empathy and compassion as Jesus taught (John 13:34).

- come to understand human nature and diverse cultures, and the need for some aspects of culture, eg. consumerism or racism, to be healed in the light of the Gospel

- engage in research in order to form well-founded judgments in keeping with Catholic Social Teaching

- listen with attention and empathy to the needs of those around them, locally and beyond

- use excellent communication skills to 'spread the good news' to their world, as Jesus commanded.

Literacy and Numeracy debates often feature in mainstream media and political life. For a Catholic school, basic skills acquisition is certainly of prime importance, but for motives of empowerment of students to become all that God destined them to be, capable and fulfilled people able to participate in the Kingdom of God, rather than primarily in response to political and economic pressure.

Language empowers.

For discussion

1. Share some of the reasons for including a study of Humanities subjects such as History, Geography and the Arts in the set curriculum. (Refer to the quote from the Church document *The Religious Dimension of Education in a Catholic School*, at the beginning of this chapter).

2. How can the faith commitment of the school influence the way the Humanities are taught?

Classroom connections: Holy Spirit School Bray Park, Queensland

The following example, taken from the Queensland 'Identity and Curriculum in Catholic Education' project, shows how the Humanities can work together in a Year 6 setting to develop learning informed by a Catholic perspective.

Three Year 6 classes planned an integrated unit using as starting points the three Catholic Social Teaching (CTS) principles: the Dignity of the Human Person, Human Equality and Stewardship of Creation, and working through English, History and Visual Arts. Resources listed for student experience and reflection included books: *Dust, Window, Where the Forest Meets the Sea, Belonging, Stolen Girl, The Lorax, Fire, Flood*, and film: *Rabbit Proof Fence, Stolen Girl*.

Teacher reflections on the outcomes of this unit included the following:

Catholic Social Teaching (CTS) provided an excellent framework for discussing and analysing news items and events in the media and students showed greater confidence when dealing with controversial issues (e.g. asylum seekers).

Teachers were able to address social and personal issues within the classroom among students. Students were continually making links across the curriculum (e.g. in Geography/Health). Teachers noted that students need an opportunity to discuss and engage with CST in different contexts to allow deeper understanding of concepts.

History

Teachers should guide the students' work in such a way that they will be able to discover a religious dimension in the world of human history. As a preliminary, they should be encouraged to develop a taste for historical truth, and therefore to realize the need to look critically at texts and curricula which, at times, are imposed by a government or distorted by the ideology of the author. The next step is to help students see history as something real: the drama of human grandeur and human misery. The protagonist of history is the human person, who projects onto the world, on a larger scale, the good

and the evil that is within each individual. History is, then, a monumental struggle between these two fundamental realities, and is subject to moral judgments. But such judgments must always be made with understanding. *The Religious Dimension of Education in a Catholic School* # 58

In a Catholic school context, teachers of history develop historical literacy with their students. The knowledge and skills acquired can help students learn to:

- 'read the signs of the times' by interpreting how history was shaped in past times and is being shaped now by human responses to changing realities

- imagine a better future, drawing on knowledge of both the rich heritage and the mistakes of the past

- understand the influence of Christianity and the great religions on the course of human history

- identify remarkable role models from history

- see the connections with science in the evolution of the cosmos as the 'Big History' of God's creation during more than 13 billion years, with human history the most recent stage of that evolution

The Australian History curriculum can be enriched by the addition of resources and learning strategies that provide an understanding of the role religion and spirituality have played in human history, and tools for interpreting the various worldviews that have dominated history.

One way to do this could be by adding additional 'Elaborations' based on a faith perspective, to those existing in the online curriculum. (Note: 'Elaborations' is a technical term used in the official Australian curriculum, which can be interpreted to mean 'teaching strategies for enrichment' or equivalent).

This is illustrated as follows for Year 2, Year 6 and Year 9.

Australian History Curriculum: Additions

Year 2 Level:

- including the local Catholic Parish Church, or the Cathedral, as an example of a 'building of significance'. Learn when and why it was built. Who donated the funds? What did that say about the importance of the building to them? Interview a parishioner who was involved in building the Church, or whose ancestors were. Ask: Do people still need places where they can meet to pray and honour God? Visit the local Church. Describe its structure, atmosphere etc.

- discussing how God gave us gifts to think, make, imagine and how we need to develop those gifts.

- Discussing what toys you could create to play with if you lived without any internet and without electricity, in a place far from the city. For example, could you 'create' a football from scraps? How? Build a cubby from branches? What effect would it have on you to have to 'create' your own fun? Discussing: Do we have too many toys? Debating the topic: *Bought toys are better than homemade ones.*

- Writing a prayer thanking God for technology and asking that we be helped to use it sensibly and wisely.

Year 6 History:

- introducing readings from *The Happiest Refugee* (2010, Allen and Unwin), by comedian and high profile Australian and former refugee, Ahn Do, who fled Vietnam by boat in the 1970's. Ahn Do tells how his religious faith, Jesuit schooling and his uncle, a Jesuit Priest, helped to sustain himself and his family in the struggle to escape and settle to make a home in Australia

- researching the life of Bishop Vincent Long, who has a similar background as a refugee. Bishop Long was appointed Bishop of Parramatta, where the most dense resettlement of refugees in Australia has occurred. He is an influential voice in advocating for justice.

- using the Social Justice Sunday Statement *For Those Who've Come Across the Seas* (2015), published by the Australian Catholic Bishops, to expand knowledge and understanding of the plight of refugees and the role they have played in Australia's life and development.

Year 9 Level:

- introducing *Rerum Novarum*, 'Of New Things', the encyclical by Pope Leo XIII, the first of the great Catholic modern social teachings, addressing the condition and rights of workers in the late 19th century. (Refer to Centre for Concern, summary article for students). [32]

- studying the foundation of the St Vincent de Paul Society in Paris by Frederic Ozanam in 1833. [33].

- viewing extracts from the movie *Les Miserables*

- drawing on a series of lessons on the Oxfam website addressing Social Justice and the Industrial Revolution [34]

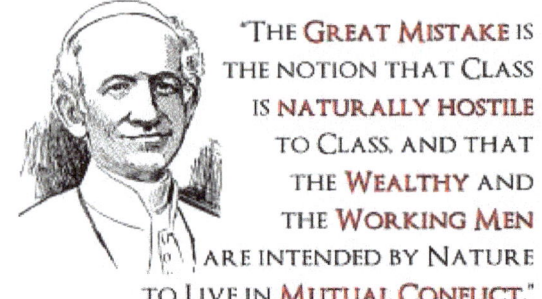

Geography

Teachers and students of Geography in a Catholic school context might ask some questions related to faith, ethics and social justice, for example:

- how can humans respect the earth and its eco-systems?

- how can people live more harmoniously with the earth in sustainable communities that respect human dignity?

- why do some cultures have so many people who live in abject poverty while other cultures prosper?

- how could the earth's resources be more equitably shared among the world's peoples?

The 'Catholic Identity and Curriculum in Catholic Education' Queensland project has mapped the Australian Geography curriculum to include connections with the themes of Catholic Social Teaching, and also utilising teaching/learning strategies developed by Caritas Australia.[35] The following is one illustrative example of how this has been done.

In Year 3 Geography and Catholic Social teaching, (ACHGK016, (ACHGK019) include for study:

- 'The location of Australia's neighbouring countries and their diverse characteristics

- The similarities and differences between places in terms of their type of settlement, demographic characteristics and the lives of the people who live there

Activities related to these areas of study and to the Catholic Social Teaching, 'The Preferential Option for the Poor', are suggested as follows:

- Explore choices that result in a more just and compassionate world.

- (Discuss ingredients of 'full and beautiful' life; word cloud; Think-Pair-Share in response to comic; record understandings of 'fair')

- Identify how acting fairly is an important way to show God's love.

- (Read comic; investigate scriptural texts; jigsaw activity)

- Consider Jesus' teaching on the poor.

- (Review comic; consider meaning of 'poor'; connect Jesus' teachings to attitudes and actions today)

Students investigate the work of Caritas Australia. (Complete research table on Caritas' work in Brazil; Explore links between this and scripture directives)

(Note: Bracketed activities, including the 'comic' referred to, are found at: http://www.caritas.org.au/learn/catholic-social-teaching

Economics and Business Studies

Money must serve, not rule! The Pope loves everyone, rich and poor alike, but he is obliged in the name of Christ to remind all that the rich must help, respect and promote the poor. I exhort you to generous solidarity and to the return of economics and finance to an ethical approach, which favours human beings. Pope Francis. *Evangelii Gaudium* # 58

In economies and business, Catholic school students can seek answers to ethical and moral questions, such as:

- How can economic policies respect the dignity of each human person and the pursuit of the common good?

- How do I respond to the following words of Pope Francis?

Business is a vocation, and a noble vocation, provided that those engaged in it see themselves challenged by a greater meaning in life; this will enable them truly to serve the common good by striving to increase the goods of this world and to make them more accessible to all. Pope Francis, *Evangelii Gaudium*, # 203

The resources for secondary students produced by Caritas Australia and Catholic Agency for Overseas Development (CAFOD) in Britain, are helpful in discussing topics such as poverty and wealth and the 'Sustainable Development Goals'. [36]

Pope Francis' teaching in *Laudato Si* explores the themes of economics and sustainability and the relationships between the so-called developing and developed countries. A practical guide to the encyclical, *Care for our Common Home: An Australian Group Reading Guide to Laudato Si* is available for senior students and teachers and is particularly relevant for use in Geography, Economics, Science and Religious Education classes.[37]

The Arts

Literary and artistic works depict the struggles of societies, of families, and of individuals. They spring from the depths of the human heart, revealing its lights and its shadows, its hope and its despair. The Christian perspective goes beyond the merely human, and offers more penetrating criteria for understanding the human struggle and the mysteries of the human spirit. # 55 Furthermore, an adequate religious formation has been the starting point for the vocation of a number of Christian artists and art critics. *The Religious Dimension of Education in a Catholic School* **# 61**

Students of Drama, Music, Dance, Media Arts and Visual Arts can express their own growing understanding of life as well as capture aspects of the worlds of culture/s, past and present through their study of the arts. Through research, expression, performance and creative processing, designing, making and creating, students share in some way the creative genius of God. They explore the beauty, terror, evil, love and positive achievements of humanity and of culture.

Jean Houston explains:

> A high-touch education—holistic, integrated, arts-centered—calls forth the natural splendour inherent in every child's mind and body. Human beings contain far more images, ideas, stories, information, feelings, and, of course, consciousness than any computer. In a sense, we humans are meta-computers with the entire cosmos as our hard drive and our body-minds the screen for its unfolding. Jean Houston, *Transformational Education* KOSMOS, Journal of Cultural transformation, Fall/Winter 2014

Students who have been recently settled as refugees in Australian schools have processed through Drama, Music, Visual Arts and creative writing their experiences of alienation, violence, fear, grief and joy as they made the journey from situations of oppression in their beloved homeland to the relative safety and peace of a new and often puzzling country. This is seen for example in the work of Treehouse Theatre in Sydney.

Young people tormented by bullying have been able to express their emotions and needs through the Arts.

In a Catholic school, teachers, aware of the Gospel values of human dignity, compassion and forgiveness, can help students' develop self-knowledge, sensitivity to others and compassion through the Arts.

Container artwork, St Anthony's School Riverside, Tasmania.

Classroom connections: Guilford Young College, Hobart

Year 11 and 12 students drew from primary sources to research the life of Blessed Frédéric Ozanam, founder of the St Vincent de Paul Society, drafting a detailed script for a new play, 'Frédéric'. With their teacher as producer, the students presented the production across the state of Tasmania and it remains a valuable resource for the St Vincent de Paul Society, testimony to how profoundly this group of students had been able to interpret the life and work of a young Catholic lawyer and his followers at the time of the French Revolution, responding to the great needs of the poor then, and, through the St Vincent de Paul Society, ever since. In speaking with the young performers, the depth of their reflection on Frédéric's life and work and the lasting influence of that on their own lives were clearly evident.

In the following example, Drama, Dance and the Visual Arts, English and Religious Education worked in sync to develop whole school intercultural understanding and Gospel compassion.

Classroom connections: St Virgil's College, Hobart

Through a partnership with Mary Rice Centre (MRC) in Kenya, students were invited to live out the College commitment to 'Advocacy rather than charity'.

The project hoped to expand the notion that the College connection with Mary Rice Centre went beyond the focal fund-raising day, and beyond the domain of the Religious Education Department, to affect the whole school community through their total learning programs.

Several activities were incorporated into Grade 3-10 classes, across a number of subject areas, including Art, Drama, Dance, English and Religious Education to familiarise the students with Mary Rice Centre. Activities included a web quest/co-operative quiz using the MRC website; the sharing of stories about MRC; listening to and looking at photos and video of the immersion experiences of staff who have visited MRC. Students made African shields in Art classes, some of which were gifted to the MRC. They watched a short YouTube clip of the Kibera slum and completed a 'see, think, wonder' reflection. They learnt Kenyan songs and dance.

Classroom connections: De La Salle College, Cronulla, NSW

The Clancy Prize for Religious Art

The Clancy Religious Art exhibition is held annually in Sydney Catholic schools.

The words from the Canticle of St Francis, 'Be praised my lord for the gift of Life; for changing dusk and dawn; for touching scent and song' inspired Rachel Johnson from De La Salle College Cronulla in her painting of St Francis. Students involved and visitors to the exhibition over many years have been profoundly affected by the ways in which students have linked art and belief.

Rachel Johnson and her painting.

A Cosmic Mural

Year 3 students at St Brigid's Primary School New Norfolk in Tasmania worked on a mural, pasting their individual 'doodle' pen and ink circle drawings onto a colourful background to depict the cosmos as God's creation. The were able to explain to me with passion and pride their learning about the universe and the fun they had in art lessons getting it all together. Art, Science and Religious Education worked together to leave a lasting impression of joy, awe and wonder for these young learners.

Jean Houston has been an advocate for transformative education, especially though the creative arts, and writes:

> In the course of my work with United Nations agencies and other international programs, I have observed many schools and many styles of learning the world over, and the best of them, the ones to which children run in delight and expectation, are those where learning is creation, performing, thinking across subjects, exploring ideas through images, sounds, songs, dances, and artistic expression. There, children become conscious participants in their own unfolding. Yes, they continue to read, and write, and cipher, but they are also encouraged to imagine, dream, and expand the limits of the possible. Jean Houston, *Transformational Education* KOSMOS, Journal of Cultural transformation. Fall/Winter 2014

'Expanding the limits of the possible' is a phrase reminiscent of Jesus' dream to make visible the Kingdom of God among us through the spiritual transformation of individual lives and of our world. St Paul calls humans, 'God's work of art', (Gal. 2). The Arts can have a unique role in holistic human growth and fulfilment, in uncovering and expressing the beauty of creation, through the 'delight' and expectation' they evoke.

For discussion

1. Noting the examples cited above, share an example of a 'God moment', a moment of insight and wonder, or a spiritually significant learning, your students have gained as they engaged in an area of the Humanities.

2. In education funding, the Arts are sometimes considered a 'luxury'. Comment on this view.

CHAPTER 7

Sciences, Maths, Health/PE

School programming has given increased attention to science and technology. Those teaching these subject areas must not ignore the religious dimension. They should help their students to understand that positive science, and the technology allied to it, is a part of the universe created by God. There can be no conflict between faith and true scientific knowledge; both find their source in God. *The Religious Dimension of Education in a Catholic School # 56*

Science and technology

In the sciences and technology, through forming hypotheses, testing, designing, coding, interpreting and drawing conclusions, students studying in a Catholic school context can learn to make sense of their world and develop an ethical framework as they grow towards:

- Understanding and appreciating God's creation
- Dreaming better futures through applied science and technology for our planet, its people and species
- Designing programs, products and systems that are respectful of human dignity and are environmentally sustainable

Student at work in the St Mary's College 'Women in Science' laboratory.

- Challenging human development that is not ethical
- Working for the health and well being of all
- Basing scientific work on highest ethical standards

Linking Catholicity and Science

Creative ways to bring Catholicity into dialogue with Science include for example, linking the curriculum with the themes of Catholic Social Teaching, which were introduced in Chapter 1. The Queensland project, 'Identity and Curriculum in Catholic Education', introduced in earlier chapters has mapped the Australian Science Curriculum against the themes of Catholic Social Teaching for Lower, Middle and Upper Primary and for Lower and Middle Secondary levels. Activities related to the national curriculum are matched with suggested activities drawn from Caritas, the Global Education Project and the Edmund Rice Centre.[38] An example follows.

Classroom connections: St Columban's College Caboolture, Queensland

In a Biology Unit 'Human impact on eco-systems', teachers agreed to link the Catholic Social Teaching principle, 'Stewardship of Creation' into the curriculum Priority, 'Sustainability', taking account also of the curriculum General Capability, 'Ethical Understanding'.

Passages from Pope Francis' encyclical *Laudato Si: Care for our Common Home*, that related to the impact of humans on ecosystems were introduced. As the APRE put it, 'The intention was to make the connection between what the Pope is saying and what's happening in our world... we are trying to raise awareness of the social and ethical teaching of the Church'.

The teachers and students could be said to be 'doing theology' as they made the connections between faith (represented here by the body of Catholic Social Teaching) and culture (the Biology topic being studied *is* an aspect of culture).[39]

Linking Science and Religious Education

An example described in Chapter 9, taken from St Mary's College in Hobart, shows how related Science and Religious Education topics can be taught concurrently, so that the relevant connections can be made for students through both disciplines. For example in this case, genetics and the origins of the universe were being treated both in Science and RE at the same time.

This is particularly powerful as a way to avoid compartmentalising knowledge and understandings, and showing how faith taught in RE and aspects of culture, found here through Science, can mutually influence student learning for greater understanding. This is an opportunity for the Gospel to shine through a holistic approach to the 'set' curriculum. Good teachers are alert to recognising such opportunities.

Another obvious example is linking the teaching of creation in the Book of Genesis in RE classes and linking it with the science of 'The Universe Story' and 'Big History'. Fr Denis Edwards, eco-theologian, writes:

> We are ultimately born from the Big Bang 13.7 billions years ago; we are made from the stars. The atoms of carbon and other elements that make up our bodies are made from stardust. We carry within us a story of life that goes back to our human ancestors in Africa, and ultimately back to the first microbial forms of life 3.7 billion years ago.[40]

Pope Francis addressed the Pontifical Academy of Sciences on this topic stating that God is not some kind of 'a magus, with a magic wand able to make everything.... The beginning of the world is not the work of chaos.... but derives directly from a supreme Origin that creates out of love. The Big Bang, which nowadays is posited as the origin of the world, does not contradict the divine act of creating, but rather requires it'.[41]

'Teachable moments' in Science

Frequently a discovery or piece of exciting scientific news is featured and captivates the interest of teachers and students alike. Such events offer 'teachable moments' that can lead to fruitful classroom discussion.

Classroom connections: A 'Teachable moment'

'Accidental' Science

On one afternoon, I was doing my rounds of the school playground and I recall a mother who was a qualified scientist, waiting to collect her Grade 2 child. She excitedly drew my attention to a particularly interesting, vividly coloured fungus she spotted in the school garden, which she then brought in to her child's classroom to show the teacher. The wonder and awe on the children's faces was reflected that afternoon in a thankyou prayer to God for creation before they (reluctantly) left this latest juicy discovery sitting on the teacher's desk until the next morning, by which time some of the bright sparks had already found the specimen online and had facts ready for 'Show and Tell'.

The following is another example of a 'teachable moment' in practice where the recent scientific discovery of 'Gravitational Waves' in outer space was opened up for discussion in a classroom setting.

The teacher was in fact applying the steps in 'doing theology', the 'See, judge, act' process of reflection outlined in Chapter 5.

Classroom connection: Seeing, Judging, Acting

Gravitational Waves

1. Seeing the Evidence: Describing and analysing the discovery of Gravitational Waves featured online, a big news item early in 2016. Asking: What has happened here? Stating the scientific facts of the discovery (after viewing it online) in as simple terms as possible, based on the evidence presented. Asking, for example: What do we make of these events? How are the scientists seeing this? Are they playing God? What feelings do you experience when you hear about this discovery? [42]

2. Responding to the Evidence: Deepening understanding: Asking for example: What concepts and values associated with Catholic belief are relevant to this discovery? Does it enhance or threaten faith in God? How can faith respect the role of science to grow human understanding of the universe, while teaching that God is its loving originator? What is my response to the vastness of the universe and the potential it holds still to be discovered? Does any of this matter or my life? For humanity? For science? Is there a Psalm or other scriptural passage that expresses the magnificence of the Universe?

3. Acting on the Discovery: Coming to Decision and Action: Asking for example: How can I/we respond and act as a result of this new learning? The discussion could be followed up with response writing, or debate on the value or otherwise of deep space exploration. At an assembly students could share their learning and invite the school community to join in praying Psalm 8 in praise of creation.

For discussion

1. Read the Vatican quote at the head of this chapter. Comment on your response to the sentence, 'There can be no conflict between faith and true scientific knowledge; both find their source in God'.

2. Share a 'God moment' students have experienced through Science classes at your school.

Mathematics

Through their Mathematics, as students learn to compute, calculate, solve problems and find correct solutions, they can also grow towards:

- A sense of wonder at the pattern and order in the universe created by God and express gratitude for the wonder of creation

- Calculating how the world's resources can be distributed more justly as a loving God intended

- Suggesting ways to help solve the problems of sustainable production to respect 'The Earth our Common Home' as Pope Francis has sub-titled his encyclical on the environment

- Using data analysis to suggest more ecologically sustainable ways of operating economic and social systems

- Recognizing the importance of just banking and economic systems as Catholic Social Teaching recommends

- Learning the value of budgeting to 'Live simply so that all may simply live' as the Gospel invites Christians through the Beatitudes

- Making the connections of Mathematics with Technology, Engineering and Science in developing a better world

The Queensland 'Identity and Curriculum in Catholic Education' project, has extensively mapped the Australian Mathematics curriculum (from Lower Primary to Lower Secondary levels) to take account of Catholic Social Teaching as a relevant resource. There are linked activities at each stage of the curriculum that help students make these connections. Two examples follow from the Australian Curriculum, Years 5 and 6 Mathematics.

Outdoor Maths, Year 4, St Brigid's School Wynyard, Tasmania.

Classroom connection: Maths for Life

1. Preparing a school budget. The themes of 'Human Dignity', 'Participation', 'Common Good', 'Inclusion and opportunity' are invoked as students use the four mathematical operations and a spreadsheet to engage in problem solving. (Ref. ACMNA100 and ACMNA291). The strategy suggested is that the students imagine they are running a school in a developing country, and preparing a simple budget on limited financial resources that can best meet the needs of the local students.

2. Grade 5/6 students are introduced to 'Micro-financing' through cooperative ventures in India, Indonesia, the Philippines and the Solomon Islands that aim to strengthen the financial independence and dignity of the poor through co-operative ventures.

These are two examples of scores of strategies linked to Catholic Social Teaching that are suggested in the Identity and Curriculum in Catholic Education project across the scope of the Mathematics curriculum. [43]

For discussion

Science without an ethic has brought humankind to the brink of ecological disaster and nuclear destruction. Scientists who were there tell when the Manhattan Project began in 1942, commissioned to create the first atomic bomb, no one present ever asked, 'Should we be doing this?' or, 'Who will suffer?', but only, 'How will we do it?' Scientific knowledge, devoid of ethic, will eventually destroy us. Thomas Groome, *Educating for Life*

▲ What are the implications of this statement for teachers of Science?

Health/PE

Through Health studies and Physical Education, students in a Catholic school context can come to appreciate that:

- human beings are wondrously made in the image and likeness of God, precious in God's sight

- the body is the 'Temple of the Holy Spirit', the sole medium through which human life can flourish and deserves respect and care at every stage of human development

Brisbane Catholic Education has mapped the Australian Health and PE Curriculum (HPE) to take account of Catholic faith and teaching, using the online Australian Curriculum portal developed by the Australian Curriculum, Assessment and Reporting Authority (ACARA).

An additional icon (a cross small cross 🌐), has been introduced at various points in the mapping, where a relevant Catholic belief, doctrine or interpretation, or an associated teaching/learning strategy, has been

School gardens can teach children the value of good nutrition, St Brigid's Wynyard, Tasmania.

added to the online curriculum. The effect is that the same public curriculum 'look' is retained, but with the addition of a Catholic perspective.

An example of how this looks at Foundation, Year 5/6 and Year 9 follows.

Classroom connections: Mapping PE/Health

1. At 'Foundation' Level: A Catholic perspective includes some 'Foundational Theological Concepts': The Person; Sexuality; Love; Loving Ethically & Living Safely (These are hyperlinked to an 'Overarching Theological Background' document). Students will come to understand that: Our bodies are gifts. Each and every life is a true gift and unique image of God. Relevant Scripture passages are suggested for Queensland teachers to use as resources.

2. Health/PE at Year 5 and 6 level: The 'Catholic Perspective' link includes the following: Students learn that humans are made in God's image and are whole in body, mind and spirit. They understand that each person is to be respected, cared for and kept safe. Students examine the changes and transitions associated with their body, emotions, and relationships. They learn about gender equality, and develop their understanding of body ownership. Students use anatomical terms when learning about their body, including puberty and bodily functions. Students learn about being in loving and just relationships, and the value of living in diverse, respectful, empathetic and forgiving communities. Students apply situational awareness to recognise and react to unsafe situations. They develop responsible decision-making and practise using discernment in challenging contexts. Students use appropriate networks and helpers when reporting unsafe situations.

3. At Year 9 level: 'Catholic Perspective - Relationships & Sexuality', encourages teachers to consider how some of the following could be expressed when planning and teaching.

   - Promoting awareness of feelings and thoughts; listening to and understanding feelings; empathic perspective taking; forgiveness; responsible and compassionate direction of emotions; chastity; discernment

   - Challenging disregard for emotions; abusive language; labelling; harbouring grudges; choosing violence over peace

   - Exploring the nature and function of emotions for human thriving; love and suffering; understanding and managing strong emotions; implications of not listening to, understanding and responding proactively to one's emotions; appropriate expressions of love[44]

I recall a teacher of Health/PE once sharing with me his 'simple teaching philosophy' as he expressed it. 'I tell my students they are temples of the Holy Spirit, and treat them that way. Everything else follows'. He expressed this as a man of faith and a very fit rugby player! I've often wondered if his students understood and honoured their health and life accordingly as they grew into adult life.

For discussion

1. Share a class situation you experienced in Science, Technology, Maths or Health/PE that raised a challenging moral issue. How did you address that?

2. Identify some ways in which contemporary scientific and technological developments are helping build a better world.

CHAPTER 8

Vocational Education

… the one (Jesus) who, while being God, became like us in all things, devoted most of the years of his life on earth to manual work at the carpenter's bench. The truth that by means of work humans participate in the activity of God himself, the Creator, was given particular prominence by Jesus Christ- the Jesus at whom many of his first listeners in Nazareth 'were astonished, saying, "Where did this man get all this? What is the wisdom given to him? Is not this the carpenter?"' (Mark 6:2-3) For Jesus not only proclaimed but first and foremost fulfilled by his deeds the 'gospel', the word of eternal Wisdom, that had been entrusted to him. Therefore this was also 'the gospel of work', because he who proclaimed it was himself a man of work, a craftsman like Joseph of Nazareth. Laborem Exercens # 26

Students study applied courses in Catholic colleges in a wide range of areas, including Construction, Food Service, Aquaculture, Viticulture, Agriculture, Animal Studies, Automotive, Cabinet Making, Carpentry, Early Childhood, Electro technology, Engineering, Hairdressing, Hospitality, Individual Support (Ageing), Plumbing.

Through vocational education in a Catholic educational setting, students can grow in understanding that:

- workers are co-creators with God, using their knowledge, skills and judgment to build a better world as they shape, make, serve, repair and invent
- work is both dignified and necessary. Jesus himself was a carpenter working with his hands to provide an essential service in his village and district
- technology, while a marvel of modern ingenuity, is a means to an end, serving the betterment of society and supporting better ways to care for the planet
- work is a vocation and can be seen as a response to God's plan for both the student and the world of work they will enter
- there is joy and fulfilment in working hard to earn a living and meeting the needs of society in a way that is generous, committed and professional
- there are a variety of gifts given to individuals by God to be recognised and nurtured for the common good of all

Applied studies require the commitment of the whole person…. hands, mind and heart, in preparation for work pathways that will help maintain and create enterprises that shape and improve the world. Students prepare to serve the needs of humanity working with built environments, machines and appliances, complex technical systems, on land, at sea and in the air.

It is vitally important that students learn to approach work with an understanding of its intrinsic dignity, the responsibilities and opportunities entailed, a moral compass and an ethical framework.

Vocational education involves the development of the student's character as well as their knowledge and skills in a particular trade or profession. Collaboration with other workers in joint projects, the care and safety of themselves and others, use of environmentally sustainable methods and materials, conscientious attention to detail and reliability, are all needed. These qualities become 'virtues' when their development is assisted by opportunities for prayer and reflection, spiritual growth and a positive approach to the power of God's Spirit, bringing life to all of creation. Students deserve to know that work is as a vital area of concern for the Church.

In an address to workers in Italy on Sept. 22, Pope Francis linked human ecology with the environment:

> Work must be combined with the preservation of creation, so that this may be responsibly safeguarded for future generations. Creation is not a good to be exploited but a gift to look after. Ecological commitment itself affords an opportunity for new concern in the sectors linked to it, such as energy, the prevention and removal of different forms of pollution, being alert to forest fires. May caring for creation and looking after humanity through dignified work be a common task. Ecology is also human ecology.
>
> (http://www.americamagazine.org/content/all-things/pope-francis-dignity-labor).

Getting it all together

Sometimes, trade training centres and schools can present as separate entities set apart from the world of the mainstream Catholic school. This could mean they are lacking some of the opportunities for symbols of faith to be visible and for spiritual development to form an integral part of school life. The impression could then be given to students and parents that faith and spirituality are irrelevant, to be confined to academic studies, and not part of the 'real world' of business and the trades.

Such an interpretation has no place in an authentically Catholic vocational education environment, which can offer a unique opportunity to bring together faith and the world of work. I noticed a tasteful wooden carved statue of St Joseph the Worker with a young Jesus at the workbench in one state-of-the-art trade training centre I visited. There is of course something very challenging about a crucifix on the wall of the workshop, reminding teachers and students of the 'tough' love Jesus was prepared to show in following his destiny in the world!

'Pastoral care' needs to have an appropriate dimension that can foster and respect faith and spiritual life within the learning centre, both personal and communal. Students are entitled to graduate appreciating that these are important aspects of life for their future.

Aquaculture Trade Training Centre, St Patrick's College, Launceston.

> *If a person sweeps streets for a living,*
> *They should sweep them as Michelangelo painted,*
> *or Beethoven composed,*
> *or as Shakespeare wrote.*
>
> Martin Luther King Jr.

Catholic approaches to trade training

An exploration of the websites of Australian Catholic trade training centres and technical colleges shows their absolute commitment to offer opportunities for training that will prepare young people for a chosen trade or profession. There is evidence of the pastoral care and personal guidance needed to accompany high quality teaching in the various vocational and trade subjects. There is also evidence that the Catholic ethos and in some cases, the religious charism, of the school provides an added dimension of motivation and inspiration.

For example, in the case of Loyola Catholic Trade Training Centre in Western Sydney, visitors to the website can note that the spirit and work of St Ignatius of Loyola is a continuing influence. The approach to education of St Ignatius is summed up in the following questions, posed by Jesuit educators since the 16th century, and remaining as guiding influences at Loyola as a twenty-first century school:

These questions have a direct relationship to the reflective process described in Chapter 5 of this guide as an aid to teachers' thinking and planning. Reflection encourages more explicitly Gospel and faith-based approaches to teaching, whether in an English class or an Automotive Engineering class, ways of teaching that are more closely aligned to Jesus' own work as teacher and champion of human dignity.

Often a few well-chosen words at assembly or in pastoral care time, or an incidental reference in a class or during a one-on-one encounter can make the difference in creating a climate that reflects the attitudes and teachings of Jesus.

The charism of St John Bosco, founder of the Salesians, friend of homeless, lawless youth in the slums of nineteenth century Naples, has found special expression in hundreds of technical schools and institutes across the globe: for example, in Bangalore, Kolkata, New Delhi and Ranchi in India, Timor-Leste, Samoa, the Philippines, South Africa, Sudan, Solomon Islands.

The Ignatian Teaching Model asks:

Context - What do we need to know about our students?

Experience - What is the best way to engage our students in learning?

Reflection - How do our students reflect more deeply on what they have learnt?

Action - How do we encourage students to move beyond knowledge to action?

Evaluation - How do we assess our student's growth in mind, heart and spirit?

(Found at: http://www.loyolacttc.catholic.edu.au/about-us)

Salesian Fr Brian Diamond, Don Bosco Technical Institute, Okhla New Delhi, India, describes his work:

> Both academic and technical education is offered by the Salesians, however the Technical schools are better known in India. The Don Bosco Technical Institute in New Delhi maintains an enrolment of 340 students (18 – 23 year old, male and female) in the government approved one or two year courses. These courses cover machine shop practices, computer science, information technology, printing and packaging, electronics and mechanics. Annually in June – July, 90 per cent of 200 trainees gain immediate employment and the remainder within six months. The graduates are motivated by employment opportunities, salaries and promotions. Surprisingly this is achieved mostly on 40 year old equipment.

Being connected

Students attending Salesian and other technical schools in Australia that remain inspired by a founder's Catholic charism can benefit greatly through communication with counterpart schools in developing countries where students are studying trade courses in challenging conditions, being offered life chances the poor would not otherwise have. Students can develop a sense of solidarity and generosity of spirit as they fund-raise, connect online and possibly even visit schools in settings similar in intent to their own, but very different in terms of available resources. Imagine a whole-school assembly where the student body could Skype students their own age engaged in trade classes in South Africa or Papua New Guinea!

In 2016, Dominic College in Hobart, a Salesian college, hosted a group of young men from the Don Bosco Technical School in Apia, Samoa, to visit their school, in what was a return visit and a truly joyous sharing of commitment to education for fullness of life. (Found at: http://www.hobart.catholic.org.au/media/news/samoan-students-wow-glenorchy)

Awareness-raising can develop in students a sense of gratitude and responsibility for the opportunities they enjoy in affluent, well-equipped technical schools, qualities that are arguably as important for students' development as are the trade-related technical skills and knowledge that will set them up for a future career path.

For discussion

1. Read the words from the Vatican document on 'Work' at the beginning of this chapter. Share your responses.

2. How does a school honour both academic and vocational courses so that students (and parents) have respect for both pathways and feel free to choose the appropriate study direction suited to the student's gifts and aptitudes?

3. How can concepts such as 'the sacredness of creation', 'human dignity', 'vocation', 'the common good', found in Catholic Social Teaching, be related to vocational education? Refer to Table 2 in Chapter 4.

Trade student at work:
St James Catholic College, Cygnet.

CHAPTER 9
Religious Education

Religion teachers are not excluded. While their primary mission must be the systematic presentation of religion, they can also be invited - within the limitations of what is concretely possible - to assist in clarifying religious questions that come up in other classes. Conversely, they may wish to invite one of their colleagues to attend a religion class, in order to have the help of an expert when dealing with some specific issue. Whenever this happens, students will be favourably impressed by the cooperative spirit among the teachers: the one purpose all of them have in mind is to help these students grow in knowledge and in commitment. *The Religious Dimension of Education in a Catholic School # 65*

Centrality of Religious Education

Each diocese has its own Religious Education curriculum approved by the bishop. Religious Education is at the heart of the total curriculum and is an important resource for all subjects. Ways must be found through shared planning, teacher conversations and shared resources to link the other disciplines with Religious Education.

Obviously this cannot be done effectively without an understanding of faith. Realistically, we acknowledge that many teachers do not have a faith background. However, when the school and parish communities work collaboratively, and teachers draw on the wealth of Church teaching, the powerful witness of the believing school community and the support of committed colleagues, much can be accomplished.

For discussion

1. Consider the quotation at the beginning of this chapter. How does this resonate with your own experience of working in a Catholic school?
2. To what extent do you think every staff member, regardless of their role, needs to take responsibility for the integrity of the school's Catholic character?

Connecting RE across the curriculum

Systems and schools are working to ensure that the Religious Education program is not isolated from the other subject areas. Obviously this is easier in a primary setting where the teacher can make the connections between what is being taught in Reading, Maths, History etc and the content of the Religious Education lessons. In secondary settings, deliberate steps need to be taken to allow for inter-disciplinary collaboration.

Classroom connections: St Anthony's School Alexander Hills, Queensland

Making the links: Primary

St Anthony's Primary School at Alexander Hills have been participants in the Queensland 'Identity and Curriculum in Catholic Education' project, developing integrated studies for Grade Three that link Religious Education, English, Science, Mathematics, Geography and Visual Arts. The 'glue' that connects the various subjects and gives a unity of purpose comes from relevant Catholic Social Teaching (See Chapter 3 for an overview of Catholic Social Teaching).

In this six week program students explore the gifts of creation through studies of Aboriginal Dreaming stories, the creation story in Genesis, Pope Francis' encyclical *Laudato Si*, Queensland environmental projects to conserve places of great beauty and significance, hands on local creek studies, climate change effects on Queensland's neighbouring Pacific Islands, statistical analysis of environmental impacts and project outcomes, literature related to the wonder of the creation and human relationships with each other and the world.

The responses from students are testimony to their engagement and growing understanding, reflection on their learning through discussion, meditation and prayer, together with decision-making leading to practical everyday actions within the school and beyond to better care for the earth and be in solidarity with the Pacific island peoples, whose homelands students had learn are being severely impacted by climate change.

Leean Bridge evaluated the experience:

> *Don't underestimate what your students can achieve. Give them a ladder and let them climb to great heights. The year threes continue to amaze me with their willingness to understand concepts that I thought might be too challenging for them, eg climate change, because they have real relevance for their lives and they want to make a difference. They want to be the Hope of Christ for a better world.*[45]

Classroom connection: St Mary's College, Hobart

Making the links: Secondary

Year 10 teachers planned for students to be able to explore some of the 'big questions' of culture and faith by timetabling for Science and Religious Education to work hand in glove.

Two topics, 'Genetics' and 'Cosmology', were studied in Science simultaneously with Religious Education topics related to 'Conscience', and to 'Creation'. This arrangement allowed for a dialogue of learning to occur for the students and teachers, as they considered the relationship between the knowledge offered through Science, with its distinctive public worldview, and the knowledge and understandings of the worldview of faith, articulated explicitly in Religious Education. It was an opportunity to understand that these subjects can complement one other in making overall sense of life and learning for students.

Some open questions were posed to students:

- What are the qualities that humans need to flourish?
- What does it mean to be both an individual and part of a community?
- How is merely surviving different from thriving?
- How is human dignity defined and what difference does it make to our decisions?

These questions were shown to be equally important in both the Science and the Religious Education classroom.

The Science Coordinator, and Head of Faith and Mission/Religious Education, worked together to see where there was a 'natural' connection between Year 10 Science and Year 10 Religious Education, to implement an additional Priority 'Catholicity', of similar ilk to the other Priorities in the Australian Curriculum. The connections are shown as follows:[46]

SCIENCE	RELIGIOUS EDUCATION
Unit: Biological Science Students learning about how the transmission of heritable characteristics from one generation to the next involves DNA and genes…	**Unit: Ethics** Students learning about the role of conscience as part of ethical decision-making, based on Catholic principles…
Unit: Earth and Space Science Students learning about the universe containing features including galaxies, stars and solar systems and the 'Big Bang' theory that can be used to explain the origin of the universe.	**Unit: Universe Story** Students learning about the context of the Catholic Church's teaching on stewardship of the Earth. Examining the scientific theory of the origin of the universe against what is claimed in Jewish and Christian texts.

Making the links: History and RE

In Year 5, a teacher can can have students research the beginnings of the Catholic Church in Australia through the life of Father Dixon, a convict Priest who came out on the First Fleet, and who said the first Masses in the colony of NSW. This study can include William Davis, Irishman, who donated land for the first Catholic Church in the new colony at Church Hill in Sydney in 1840. (This is now a Marist Father's Parish near The Rocks and an historical site of national significance). Through their History, students can learn how passionate and committed the early Catholic Irish community was in the establishment of the Catholic Church in colonial New South Wales.[47]

Making the links: curriculum mapping

Systems of Catholic education have sought ways to map the Religious Education curriculum to link with all key learning areas, and to explore how the Priorities and General Capabilities of the Australian Curriculum can be addressed through Religious Education teaching as well as through all other subjects.

An example is found from Tasmania, where the RE curriculum, *Good News for Living*, exists online in the same format as the other Australian Curriculum subjects, and is explained as follows:

The RE curriculum, 'Good News for Living', through the ACARA portal, has the same 'look' online at each Stage as the Australian Curriculum. The General Capabilities and Priorities of the Australian Curriculum are linked to each topic of the RE online curriculum, making teacher planning seamless, and visibly demonstrating how RE provides holistic learning opportunities for students that enrich and support the other curriculum areas. An additional Priority ('Catholicity') and an additional General Capability ('Wisdom') can further inform teachers as they plan linked learning programs for our students.[48]

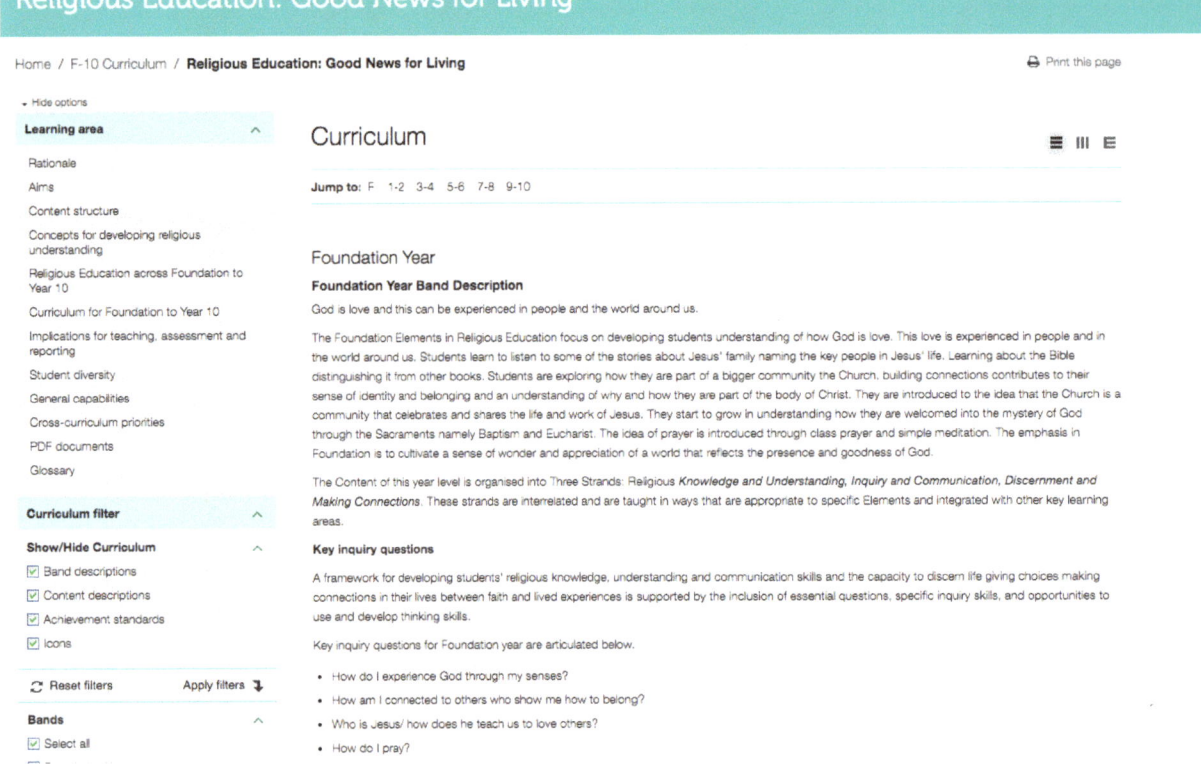

Sharing resources

Some Catholic systems of education provide extensive resource banks that are available online to support Religious Education in their schools and beyond. Many of those resources are applicable to the so-called 'secular' subjects as well.

RESource: Catholic Education Melbourne

'RESource' is an online database of resources for Religious Education and across-the-curriculum support. This data bank of resources includes 'Ethics' as one of its resource categories together with 'Scripture', 'Worship', 'Beliefs' and 'The Church'. The resources feature background briefing and interactive opportunities for teachers and students to engage in discernment as they consider various points of view to be encountered in social and religious contexts. Some related topics are, for example, Human Trafficking, Refugees, Multiculturalism, Capital Punishment, War and Peace, Censorship, Sweat Shop Labour, Carbon Taxing, Euthanasia, Wealth Distribution. Topics can resource learning in a variety of subject areas such as Economics, Commerce, Geography, History, Philosophy and Religious Education.

Found at: //www.cem.edu.au/learning-teaching/religious-education/resource/

Linking religion and life

Principals, Religious Education coordinators and Directors of Mission know that the religious knowledge and understanding, the skills in reading and interpreting scripture, the capacity to pray and engage in liturgy learned through the formal Religious Education program, need to find expression in the way we live in our daily relationships with God, self and others. Practice is needed in this to help build virtues that can last a lifetime, and overcome human tendencies towards selfishness and isolation. The bigotry and exclusion imbibed through cultural influences also need to be addressed in the light of faith.

Schools offer various opportunities for outreach to those in need to help students to make the links between religion and life, develop character, and put into practice Jesus' command, 'Love the Lord your God with your whole heart, and your neighbour as yourself'. (Matt 22:37).

Examples of practical social justice outreach programs include mini-Vinnies (junior St Vincent de Paul conferences), 'Green Guardians' (for caring for the earth in the local environment), or some equivalent.

Many schools offer experience in other countries, either through actual visits or virtually, usually associated with the charism of the school. This is seen as a way to build appreciation of diverse cultures and an understanding of how unjustly the resources of earth are distributed among the world's people. How well such initiatives can relate to Geography, History, Economics and Business Studies! Yet in some schools there is no structured collaboration between the RE and other faculties in planning and evaluating such initiatives; hence a golden opportunity is missed to bring faith and culture into dialogue.

Other examples of putting a practical face on Religious Education are seen in the exercise of hospitality and love towards the elderly or the homeless, through preparing food in Food Studies classes, or presenting music and drama that have been workshopped in classrooms, volunteer work on the Vinnies food van as part of an outreach program, sharing vegetables grown in the school garden. Many students who have had these opportunities continue from humble beginnings to be involved in works of justice, peace and ecology throughout their lives.

Classroom connections: Linking Faith and Life

The 'Make Jesus Real' (MJR) workbook and program, developed in Tasmania, is now implemented across many Australian Catholic schools. The program helps middle to upper primary students to relate to one another in a Christ-like way, using attractive, relevant language and imagery young people can relate to. Schools using the program testify to how much more positive students are both at school and at home, continuing into their later lives as well, as they develop conscience and learn to make good judgments about their own attitudes and behaviour and interactions with others. While this program is not a substitute for Religious Education, it complements formal religion lessons and supports all subjects as students learn to approach their learning in a spirit of greater cooperation and awareness of their own and others' needs.[49]

Inter-faith dialogue

Contemporary Catholic schools are often centres for interfaith dialogue and cultural understanding, as they enrol increasing numbers of students from a variety of faith backgrounds, or none.

Australian Catholic schools in capital cities have collaborated with Jewish and Islamic schools in an inter-faith dialogue of understanding and good will, making real the inter-faith studies that are part of the Studies of Religion curriculum. Such a 'dialogue of life' can form the basis for a lifelong respect for faiths and cultures that are different from one's own. What an enrichment for many other subject areas as well, as students are exposed first hand to different cultural practices and customs in History, Geography and the Arts for example.

Studies of Religion: Sydney

The organisation 'Women and the Australian Church' (WATAC) has for many years offered an annual inter-faith symposium in Parliament House NSW for senior secondary students from Sydney Catholic schools to attend. In a panel format, including a Christian, a Muslim, an Indigenous and a Jewish representative, each speaker shares an aspect of their faith journey. Students are free to engage in an open dialogue with the speakers. This has been a valuable resource for the Studies of Religion courses of the schools attending, and enriching the lives of countless young people who passed into adult life with an understanding of Catholic Church teaching on interfaith relations, as found in the Second Vatican Council document *Nostra Aetata* (1965).[50]

A resource from the Columban Fathers for schools studying inter-faith dialogue at Year 12 level can be found at: http://www.columban.org.au/assets/files/2014/the-far-east-school-resources/columban-mission-institute-interfaith-dialogue-high-school-resource.pdf

A personal experience of interfaith understanding occurred in my own professional experience when our Catholic primary school welcomed the enrolment of its first Muslim family. The father questioned whether alcohol was kept in the school. The principal explained that wine was limited to a strictly religious purpose, the celebration of the Eucharist. Through a dialogue based on trust, a mutual understanding could be reached, and the family successfully integrated into the life of the school, providing many more opportunities for interfaith dialogue as the community got to know the new students and their Muslim faith.

In 2013, Pope Francis, addressed an Albanian school, which accepted Catholic, Orthodox and Muslim children as well as several pupils of agnostic parents, declaring that 'the school is thus becoming a place for dialogue and serene exchanges to encourage attitudes of respect, listening, friendship and a spirit of collaboration'.[51]

What a difference these learning experiences can make to a young person's outlook on life as the world becomes globalised, people move across borders and cultures intermingle. Arguably nothing could be more important for building world peace and as a response to the intercultural wars of our own time than the development of intercultural understanding inspired by faith through the education of young people.

Muslim and Catholic young people in Sydney engaging in dialogue at Youth PoWR, 2015 (the Youth Parliament of World Religions), an initiative of the Columban Fathers.

Conclusion

From the nature of the Catholic school also stems one of the most significant elements of its educational project: the synthesis between culture and faith. Indeed, knowledge set in the context of faith becomes wisdom and life vision…The various school subjects do not present only knowledge to be attained, but also values to be acquired and truths to be discovered. All of which demands an atmosphere characterized by the search for truth, in which competent, convinced and coherent educators, teachers of learning and of life, may be a reflection, albeit imperfect but still vivid, of the one Teacher. In this perspective, in the Christian educational project all subjects collaborate, each with its own specific content, to the formation of mature personalities. *'The Catholic School on the Threshold of the Third Millennium' #14*

This guide set out to put a practical face on the Church's hopes for Catholic education expressed in the quotation above, seeking answers to the question: How can 'knowledge' gained through 'the subjects taught in the context of faith' become 'wisdom and life vision' for students?

I have often heard teachers and Catholic school leaders say something like, 'Yes, I understand that a Catholic way of curriculum delivery is the ideal, but HOW can it happen? Show us how'.

Some creative, practical and energetic responses from educational leaders and teachers who have been taking up the challenge are there to be seen in the examples included in this guide. There are many more to be discovered and shared in Australia and across the world.

Our forebears who founded Catholic schools in Australia built with the understanding that their schools would be distinctly 'Catholic'.

What an extraordinary opportunity and responsibility Catholic education has in this fractured world to prepare students to understand the dignity God has given them to be 'Christ-like' people, able to offer their gifts and talents to bring healing, hope and loving commitment, not only to their own family, but to the world in which they are blessed to live and work. Catholic education can help them not only in 'doing well', but in being the loving, peaceful person God destined them to be.

May Catholic schools continue to be faithful to the Gospel, a leaven in the dough of society, a light on the hill and a gift of wisdom for the young people they educate who will become in their turn the parents, the voters, the workers, and the shapers of the future.

Prayer for Teachers and Learners

Leader: We give praise and thanks to God for the opportunity to learn and to teach. We are called to follow Christ the Teacher, of whom it was said, 'They were amazed at His teaching, for He was teaching them as one having authority, and not as the scribes'. (Mark 1:28).

All: We pray that our work as teachers, bringing the curriculum to life in classrooms with our students, will be richly blessed with the Gifts of the Spirit: Wisdom, Knowledge, Understanding, Courage and a deep sense of the sacred.

1. For the privilege of sharing with young people the riches of human knowledge and experience through the curriculum we teach.

All: We thank you Lord

2. For the opportunity to marvel at the immensity of the cosmos and the natural world observed and measured through the Sciences and Mathematics.

All: We thank you Lord

3. The spirals on the seashells, the patterns of the honeycomb, the bottomless black holes in the universe, are signs of God's love and presence.

All: We praise you Creator God for sharing with us the secrets of creation.

Leader: The knowledge, skills and values for life that flow from what we learn and teach enable us to find ways to feed the hungry, care for the sick and create quality of life for all on our planet earth.

All: Lord God, we are grateful for the opportunities Catholic education offers to shape a better world.

Leader: Through languages, communication technologies and the social sciences we come to understand the many cultures of the human family. We learn to communicate with respect, to recognise truth and goodness, and to learn from those who came before us.

All: Spirit of Wisdom, help us to use the gifts of communication to bring unity and understanding to the world.

Leader: Engaged hands, hearts and minds empower learners to embrace the skills and knowledge needed to build structures and systems to house, nourish, transport and service the world.

All: Jesus, you found dignity in being a carpenter. May we honour and show gratitude for hard, honest work that serves the needs of our world.

Leader: The Creative Arts are an expression of truth, beauty, energy and love, a way to make sense of life's light and darkness and express our deepest hopes and fears.

All: Thankyou Creator God for human sensitivity and giftedness. May Music, Art, Dance and Drama be sources of joy and healing for our students.

Leader: May the curriculum we teach in Catholic schools point towards the 'Way, the Truth and the Life' (John 14:6) of Jesus for each of our students as they engage in learning for life. We make all these prayers through Jesus Christ our Lord, who not only 'taught as one having authority', but 'went about doing good' (Acts 10:38), and promised to send his Spirit to inspire us always.

Endnotes

1. Pope Francis, 'Address to Catholic Educators', Rome November, 2015

2. P Sharkey, *Educator's Guide to Catholic Identity*, (2015), Mulgrave, Vaughan Publishing.

3. Pope Francis, *Evangelii Gaudium: The Joy of the Gospel*, (2013).

4. The contemporary version of 'A Sense of the Sacred' for use in Sydney Archdiocesan Catholic schools can be found at: https://sites.google.com/a/syd.catholic.edu.au/a-sense-of-the-sacred/about

5. D'Orsa, T and J. *Catholic Curriculum: A Mission to the Heart of Young People* (2012), Mulgrave, Vaughan Publishing.

6. D'Orsa and D'Orsa, *Catholic Curriculum: A Mission to the Heart of Young People*, p 2, (2012), Mulgrave, Vaughan Publishing.

7. The Catholic identity of Catholic schools (and now parishes) has been the object of a wide-reaching study initiated in the Melbourne Archdiocese, in collaboration with Catholic University in Leuven, Belgium (KULeuven), and extending across many Australian jurisdictions. http://www.cem.edu.au/about-catholic-education/enhancing-catholic-school-identity/

8. These questions raised by Professor Therese D'Orsa for discussion with Catholic educators at a conference in Brisbane (2013) to address Catholic Curriculum. Full text found at: http://qcec.catholic.edu.au/wp-content/uploads/2015/12/Therese-D---Orsa-Catholic-Curriculum-The-Human-Faces.pdf

9. R. Rohr, O.F.M., and J. Martos, 'Eight Good Reasons for Being Catholic'. Found at: http://archgandhinagar.org/catholic-life/discovering-our-catholic-faith/being-catholic-today/eight-good-reasons-for-being-catholic/

10. A more detailed understanding of 'Culture' is found on the Broken Bay Institute website at: http://www.bbi.catholic.edu.au/books-dvds/fx-product-listing.cfm?cid=157. (Follow the link, 'Supplementary Resource to Guide for Catholic Curriculum')

11. Palmer, P. *The Courage to Teach*, p. 32, (1998), San Francisco, Jossey-Bass Inc., Publishers.

12. Palmer, P. *The Courage to Teach*, p. 107, (1998), San Francisco, Jossey-Bass Inc., Publishers.

13. A more detailed understanding of 'Dialogue' is found at the Broken Bay Institute website at: http://www.bbi.catholic.edu.au/books-dvds/fx-product-listing.cfm?cid=157. (Follow the link, 'Supplementary Resource to Guide for Catholic Curriculum')

14. For an accessible and comprehensive introduction to this body of teaching and examples of its application to the school curriculum, see the Caritas Australia website. Found at http://www.caritas.org.au/learn/catholic-social-teaching

15. Found at: http://www.socialjustice.catholic.org.au/publications/series-papers

16. Found at: http://catholicearthcare.org.au/

17. Found at: http://www.pass.va/content/scienzesociali/en.html (Pontifical Academy of Social Sciences) http://www.casinapioiv.va/content/accademia/en.html (Pontifical Academy of Sciences)

18. Found at: http://www.rec.bne.catholic.edu.au/The%20Shape%20of%20Religious%20Education/Pages/A-Catholic-View-of-Learning-and-Teaching.aspx

19. Taken from the New Zealand Catholic Education Handbook, which includes review document aims, process, dimensions and indicators. Found at: http://www.nzceo.catholic.org.nz/media/resources/2013_Special_Character_Review_update.pdf

20. Found at: http://www.nzceo.catholic.org.nz/media/resources/publications/Virtues-and-Values-in-Catholic-Schools-2014.pdf

21. Found at: http://www.kavanagh.school.nz/special-character/respect.

22. P. O'Farrell *The Catholic Church and Community in Australia*, (1977), Melbourne, Nelson.

23. A more detailed treatment of the History of Catholic Curriculum in Australia is found on the Broken Bay institute website (BBI) at: http://www.bbi.catholic.edu.au/books-dvds/fx-product-listing.cfm?cid=157. (Follow the link, 'Supplementary Resource to Guide for Catholic Curriculum')

24. Vatican, 'Towards A Pastoral Approach To Culture', (1999), para. 4.

25. *Evangelii Nuntiandi*, (1976), para. 20, Pope Paul VI.

26. The full account of the work done in working towards a Catholic curriculum in Tasmanian Catholic education can be found on the BBI website at: http://www.bbi.catholic.edu.au/books-dvds/fx-product-listing.cfm?cid=157. (Follow the link, 'Supplementary Resource to Guide for Catholic Curriculum')

27. 'Identity and Curriculum in Catholic Education' project, based at the McAuley campus, ACU, Banyo, established by the Catholic Education authorities in Queensland and some Religious Institutes. Found at: http://www.acu.edu.au/about_acu/faculties,_institutes_and_centres/education_and_arts/schools/research/identity_and_curriculum_in_catholic_education

28. The Young Christian Workers (YCW) Movement and the Young Christian Students (YCS) Movement teach the 'See Judge Act' methodology to young people as a highly effective way of linking the Gospel with their daily life challenges.

29. Found at: http://en.radiovaticana.va/news/2015/11/21/pope_francis_educate_openness_to_transcendence,_mercy/1188569.

30. Found at: http://www.acu.edu.au/about_acu/faculties,_institutes_and_centres/education_and_arts/schools/research/identity_and_curriculum_in_catholic_education/seminar_may_2016

31. Found at: https://en.wikipedia.org/wiki/Vincent_Long_Van_Nguyen

32. Found at: https://educationforjustice.org/system/files/rerumnovarum.pdf

33. Source background historical information at https://www.vinnies.org.au/page/About/History/

34. Found at: http://www.oxfam.ca/our-work/publications/educational-resources/social-justice-and-the-industrial-revolution

35. Found at: http://www.acu.edu.au/about_acu/faculties,_institutes_and_centres/education_and_arts/schools

36. Found at: CAFOD.org.uk/Education/Education-Resources

37. B Huebsch with T Hindmarsh, *Care for our Common Home: An Australian Group Reading Guide to Laudato Si*, (2015), Mulgrave, Garratt Publishing.

38. Found at: http://www.acu.edu.au/__data/assets/pdf_file/0005/772349/Science_activities.pdf

39. Detailed lesson plans available at: http://www.acu.edu.au/about_acu/faculties,_institutes_and_centres/education_and_arts/schools/research/identity_and_curriculum_in_catholic_education

40. D Edwards, *Jesus and the Natural World*, p 10, (2012), Mulgrave, Garratt Publishing.

41. Found at: http://www.news.va/en/news/francis-in-the-pontifical-academy-of-sciences-emph)

42. Ref: http://abcnews.go.com/Technology/albert-einstein-scientists-detect-gravitational-waves/story?id=36858618)

43. Found at: http://www.acu.edu.au/__data/assets/pdf_file/0004/772348/Mathematics_activities.pdf

44. The full curriculum may be found at: http://dvacara.azurewebsites.net/, following the Health and Physical Education link. (Provided with permission of BCE Executive Director Pam Betts, and advice from John McGrath, National Catholic Education Commission Education Officer: Faith Formation & Religious Education)

45. A comprehensive outline of this six-week project is found at: http://www.acu.edu.au/__data/assets/pdf_file/0009/826164/Overall_reflections_on_integration_of_CST_with_Yr_3.pdf

46. Information provided by St Mary's College Science Learning Area Coordinator, Heather Omant and Matthew Williams Head of Faith and Mission/Religious Education Learning Area Coordinator, 2016.

47. Ref: http://www.convictrecords.com.au/convicts/dixon/james/128600

48. *Good News for Living* online RE Curriculum. Found at: http://catholic.tas.edu.au/our-schools/curriculum/religious-education

49. Details about 'Making Jesus Real' can be accessed http://catholic.tas.edu.au/our-schools/curriculum/making-jesus-real or www.makejesusreal.com.au

50. Ref. http://www.watac.net/workshopsevents.php

51. Taken from 'Educating to Intercultural Dialogue in Catholic Schools: Living in Harmony for a Civilization of Love', Para. 21, (2013), Vatican City.

www.ingramcontent.com/pod-product-compliance
Lightning Source LLC
Chambersburg PA
CBHW061057170426
43195CB00024B/2983